W9-ANY-086

Sexual
Harassment

Look for these and other books in the Lucent Overview Series:

Abortion
AIDS
Child Abuse
Children's Rights
Family Violence
Gay Rights
Juvenile Crime
Sexual Harassment
Violence Against Women
Women's Rights

Sexual Harassment

by Keith McGowan

LUCENT
BOOKS

LUCENT *Overview Series*

LUCENT Overview Series

Acknowledgments are due David Haugen, Lori Shein, Christine Johnson, Johanna Striar, Shaun Cutts, Stacie Heintze, Alice Carmel, Genevieve Carmel, Susan Graves, Kim Sobel, Jeff McGowan, Kathy Hogan, Seth McGowan, Ethan McGowan, Jacob McGowan, Abuzz Technologies, the librarians at the Falmouth Public Library and the Barnstable County Law Library, Donna Joyce, and Kelly Joyce.

Library of Congress Cataloging-in-Publication Data

McGowan, Keith, 1968–
    Sexual harassment / by Keith McGowan.
        p.   cm. — (Lucent overview series)
    Includes bibliographical references and index.
    Summary: An overview of sexual harassment, including its aspects in the law, the workplace, education, and the military.
    ISBN 1-56006-507-9 (lib. bdg. : alk. paper)
    1. Sexual harassment—Juvenile literature.   [1. Sexual harassment.]   I. Title.   II. Series.
HQ1237.M34   1999
305.3—dc21   98-14683
                                                                    CIP
                                                                     AC

For Kelly Ann Joyce,
with all my love

Contents

Introduction

SEXUAL HARASSMENT PRESENTS a real and serious problem for ordinary Americans. Every year, thousands upon thousands of working women lose their jobs because they are sexually harassed in their workplaces. A similar number of secondary school students, mostly female, watch their grades drop because they are harassed in the hallways and classrooms of their schools. Further, according to the latest statistics from the Department of Defense, over eight thousand female soldiers annually receive unfairly lowered performance evaluations when they report sexual harassment within their service. These are real statistics collected by careful researchers determined to find out the facts about sexual harassment—whatever they may be. The results of their research have been clear. Sexual harassment negatively affects every sector of American society.

For this reason, calls to end sexual harassment have received the support of powerful institutional authorities. The secretary of the army has denounced sexual harassment as "abhorrent to . . . American values."[1] The Department of Education has declared sexual harassment to be "a real and serious problem in education at all levels."[2] The federal government and many state governments have enacted laws to fight sexual harassment. The American Psychological Association has called sexual harassment devastating, and the National Education Association has recommended educational programs to help people recognize, understand, and stop sexual harassment. These organizations have studied the facts about sexual harassment and, independently,

they have reached the same conclusion. The problem of sexual harassment must be addressed.

Supreme Court rulings have aided the effort to prevent and stop sexual harassment. In two landmark rulings, the Supreme Court has held unanimously that serious or repeated sexual harassment in the workplace is a form of sex discrimination in violation of the law. All nine Supreme Court justices agree on the issue of sexual harassment, even while representing starkly different judicial philosophies. This unanimity has sent a powerful message to the nation.

Identifying the problem of sexual harassment, however, has proven to be easier than solving it. Although more than two decades have passed since sexual harassment was first raised as an issue, the statistics on harassment have changed little since that time. To address the problem of sexual harassment, people will have to take a long look at the successes and failures of the past; the state of sexual harassment in today's workplaces, schools, and military bases; and the recommendations of sexual harassment researchers, experts, and activists for the future. This book provides a view into these issues.

A poster at the University of California, Berkeley, reminds passersby about the existence of sexual harassment. Schools of all levels recognize sexual harassment as detrimental to education.

1

Sexual Harassment and the Law

UNTIL THE 1970s, SEXUAL harassment was a problem without a name. The term *sexual harassment* was first used by Lin Farley in a 1974 course on women and work at Cornell University. The first people to define sexual harassment for study were Farley's associates, Karen Sauvigné and Susan Meyer, who founded the Working Women United Institute (WWUI) in 1975. Sauvigné and Meyer described sexual harassment as "any repeated and unwanted sexual comments, looks, suggestions, or physical contact that you find objectionable or offensive and that causes you discomfort on the job."[3]

One year later, a *Ladies' Home Journal* article used more vivid language to describe sexual harassment in the workplace:

> A restaurant owner grabs a waitress' rear whenever she passes the cash register. A police officer makes advances to the woman cop with whom he shares a patrol car. A politician bombards his female staff with vulgar remarks about their breasts. An executive offers his secretary to visiting buyers when he isn't chasing her around the desk himself.[4]

In 1975, Sauvigné and Meyer surveyed 155 working women. The results were telling. Seventy percent of the women surveyed had experienced sexual harassment. A full 56 percent had been physically harassed. Sauvigné and Meyer's pioneering survey was quickly followed by others. A survey at the United Nations found that half of the women and nearly a third of the men had "experienced or witnessed" sexual harassment. In a survey at Michigan State University, 73 percent of the female custodians responded that sexual harassment was a problem.

In January 1976, *Redbook* published a questionnaire asking women "How do you handle sex on the job?"[5] Of the nine thousand women who responded, eighty-one hundred reported experiencing sexual harassment. Legal scholar and feminist Catharine MacKinnon explains why the *Redbook* survey was so important: "[B]efore this survey, it would have been difficult to convince a person of ordinary skepticism that [eighty-one hundred] American women existed who would report experiencing sexual harassment at work."[6]

For MacKinnon and many others, these surveys made an important point. Sexual harassment, the surveys suggested, was something that women faced as a group. It was not an individual problem; it was a problem of society at large. In

'... We need to discuss your memo on sexual harassment in the workplace... How about over dinner tonight?...'

Redbook, in *Ladies' Home Journal*, in public forums, and in the press, women maintained that sexual harassment was an issue of women's equality in the workplace.

Sex discrimination

"One would expect strong legal remedies to be available to victims of such an experience—and severe penalties to be imposed on harassing employers," wrote Letty Cottin Pogrebin, a founding editor of *Ms.* magazine, in her 1976 *Ladies' Home Journal* article. Pogrebin noted, however, that it was "not . . . clear at the moment" if such legal remedies were in place.[7]

During the 1970s, a handful of women pushed sexual harassment into the courts. These were ordinary women, unknown to the public: a payroll clerk for the Environmental Protection Agency, two clerical workers at the Bausch & Lomb Company, a secretary working for Saxon Business Products, and a secretary at the Public Service Electric & Gas Company, among others. Each of these women had suffered losses due to sexual harassment. Several of them had been fired when they refused to have sex with their bosses. Independently, these women brought suits against their employers.

When sexual harassment moved into the courtroom, it became a question for judges to resolve, with help from lawyers, legal scholars, and the government. Women's magazines and women's rights activists had set the tone. Sexual harassment was a wrong endured by countless women trying to work with men as equals. But the courts had to answer a narrower question. Was sexual harassment illegal?

Diane Williams was one of many women to argue, in court, that sexual harassment was illegal. Her lawsuit was typical of sexual harassment cases during the time period. Williams, a public information specialist for the Department of Justice, had rejected the sexual advances of her supervisor, Harvey Brinson. After her rejection, Brinson harassed and intimidated Williams at work and, three months later, he fired her.

To argue her case, Williams depended on a law passed by Congress a decade earlier, the Civil Rights Act of 1964. Title VII of the Civil Rights Act of 1964 made it illegal for employers to treat women and men differently at work. In legal terms, Title VII of the act made it illegal for employers to discriminate (distinguish) on the basis of sex.

Brinson had certainly treated Williams differently than a man, Williams argued in her lawsuit. His actions amounted to an extra job requirement—a requirement that she have sex with him as a part of her job. Brinson would not have placed this requirement on a male employee, contended Williams. A man could have held the job without incident.

In an historic ruling, federal judge Charles R. Richey agreed. Williams had faced "an artificial barrier to employment," he ruled, "placed before one [sex] and not the other."[8] Judge Richey reasoned that this barrier was no different from any rule that made it more difficult for a woman to hold a job.

The first rulings to protect women from sexual harassment on the job were handed down in the 1970s. Sexual harassment was deemed a form of sex discrimination and was therefore illegal.

Examining the Civil Rights Act of 1964, Richey found that the act did indeed apply to this case. Brinson's behavior was "sex discrimination within . . . Title VII of the Civil Rights Act of 1964," Richey ruled.[9] Brinson had treated Williams unfairly at work because she was a woman, and therefore he had violated the law.

Quid pro quo sexual harassment

Today, Brinson's actions would be called "quid pro quo" sexual harassment. Quid pro quo (something for something, in Latin) occurs when a supervisor wants to trade a job, job benefits, a promotion, or a raise, in exchange for sex. Usually, in quid pro quo sexual harassment cases, the employee rejects the supervisor's sexual demands and suffers a loss. This is what happened to Williams. She rejected Brinson's advances and lost her job.

Judge Richey's ruling would set the standard in the upcoming years. Other federal courts joined Richey, declaring that quid pro quo sexual harassment was indeed a form of sex discrimination. Sexually harassed women won a string of legal victories. By the end of the 1970s, many courts had accepted quid pro quo sexual harassment as a form of sex discrimination.

But the majority of sexual harassment complaints, voiced in magazines and surveys, did not fit the legal definition of quid pro quo harassment. Demands for sex were only one type of harassment. Women experienced physical harassment—pinching and grabbing. Women experienced leering. Women experienced verbal harassment—comments about their breasts, their looks, and their anatomy. Men talked to women about the size of their penises and their sexual ability. Even if a supervisor demanded sex, the employee could only claim quid pro quo harassment if she was fired or punished for refusing such demands.

While some women *were* fired for complaining of this sexual conduct, and others simply quit, most remained at their jobs, enduring harassment with no end in sight. Laws against quid pro quo harassment did not address this issue. Sexual harassment, at its core, was not about being unemployed. Women wanted equal treatment *while* they worked, not just compensation after they were fired.

Hostile environment sexual harassment

In 1980, the government stepped into the legal debate on the side of women's rights activists. The Equal Employment Opportunity Commission (EEOC) was the government agency charged with enforcing workplace discrimination laws. Under the leadership of chair Eleanor Holmes Norton, the EEOC endorsed a new category for sexual harassment claims: "hostile environment" sexual harassment. Hostile environment harassment occurred when an employee faced an intimidating, hostile, or offensive environment at work, directed at the employee because of the employee's sex. When sexual harassment created a hostile environment or interfered with an employee's job performance, explained the EEOC, it should be considered sex discrimination, even if the employee was not fired or denied a job benefit.

Working women immediately benefited from the government's leadership role. Sandra Bundy was one of these women. Bundy worked for the Washington, D.C., Department of Corrections as a vocational specialist, finding jobs for former criminal offenders. She fended off repeated advances from two supervisors. When she complained to a higher level manager, he told her that "any man in his right mind would want to rape you," and requested that she "begin a sexual relationship with him in his apartment."[10] Bundy was never fired, but she filed suit nonetheless.

Since Bundy had not suffered an economic loss, her case could not be considered quid pro quo harassment. She

Eleanor Holmes Norton (right) of the EEOC introduced the hostile environment harassment claim in the early 1980s.

was not fired for rejecting her supervisors. However, she did have to endure their behavior as a condition of her work, and her environment at work was threatening. Bundy's case fell into the hostile environment category. Her job was severely affected because she was a woman.

Bundy's case was decided in January 1981—a brief two months after the EEOC endorsed hostile environment harassment claims—by the D.C. Circuit Court of Appeals. The court found in her favor. Sexual harassment amounted to discrimination, wrote Chief Judge J. Skelly Wright, echoing the EEOC's definition of hostile environment sexual harassment, "regardless of whether the complaining employee lost any tangible job benefits as a result of discrimination." [11]

One year later, in *Henson v City of Dundee*, the Eleventh Circuit Court used more powerful language to denounce hostile environment sexual harassment. Nobody should be expected to "run a gauntlet of sexual abuse," the court declared, "in return for the privilege of being allowed to work and make a living." [12]

The court went on to explain hostile environment claims in detail. Employees had only to show that they faced a "pattern of sexual harassment" at work that created a hostile environment. "There is no requirement that an employee . . . prove in addition that she has suffered tangible job detriment," the court explained. [13]

By accepting hostile environment claims in *Bundy* and *Henson*, the federal courts more adequately addressed the grievances of thousands of women who were intimidated on the job. The central question of sexual harassment in the law had been answered. Sexual harassment was illegal, even if the employee kept her job, because women and men had the legal right to equality in the workplace.

Judicial standards

In the early 1980s, the courts turned toward subtler legal questions. The course of the law was still driven by employees who took their claims to court. However, the law was also shaped by the judiciary's need to create standards of judgment that every court could use. Throughout the

decade, judges would make critical decisions as they ruled, case by case, on claims of sexual harassment.

Quid pro quo harassment cases had been clear-cut. It was easy to measure the harm done to an employee who had unfairly lost her job. But hostile environment cases were much more difficult for the courts to handle. The harm in hostile environment cases was measured by words such as *intimidation, insult, offense,* and *abuse.* Courts needed a way to measure these difficult concepts.

The courts decided to use the phrase "severe or pervasive," which means, in plain terms, serious or repeated. To win a hostile environment lawsuit, employees would have to show that the harassment was serious enough or repeated enough to affect their jobs. In each case the court would ask, "Was the harassment severe or pervasive?"

Severe or pervasive

Physical harassment was almost always considered serious, or severe, enough to meet the legal standards for sexual harassment. If an employee was grabbed, fondled, pushed against a wall, or kissed, even once, the courts usually held that the workplace had become a hostile environment. After such an incident, the courts understood, the employee may not wish to return to work at all.

For example, in *Barrett v Omaha National Bank*, one incident was enough to meet the legal standard of severe or pervasive. Deanna Barrett's coworker rubbed and touched her "in an offensive manner, while they were inside a vehicle from which she could not escape."[14] Because of the physical nature of the harassment, one incident was enough to affect her job.

Verbal harassment was usually considered less severe. A sexual slur, courts ruled, would not be enough to state a legal claim. One verbal insult did not amount to discrimination. However, judges recognized that an employee's workplace could become intolerable if the employee encountered verbal harassment day in and day out. Courts sometimes called this a pattern of sexual harassment. When harassment involved verbal abuse, the courts would ask, "How often did the verbal abuse occur?"

For example, when Rita Coley worked for the Consolidated Rail Corporation, her boss confronted her with talk about her "boobs," her menstrual cycle, and more than once he asked her suggestively, "When are you going to do something nice for me?" He also told her that she had better do something "nice" for him soon or he was going to "get mean."[15] Coley had no problem proving a pattern of sexual harassment in court.

A denied claim

Not all cases, however, met what most believed to be a reasonable standard. The sexual harassment lawsuit filed by Patricia J. Hollis, a junior data entry clerk at Fleetguard, Inc., was neither severe nor pervasive enough to stand up in the courtroom. Hollis's coworker had propositioned her four times over a period of four months. Afterwards, he acted unfriendly toward her and avoided her. Once, she reported, he yelled at her in front of other employees. The court that heard Hollis's case did not believe her working environment was hostile or intimidating enough to state a legal claim of sexual harassment. Hollis's workplace may have been uncomfortable, but it was not discriminatory. Her claim was denied.

Unwelcome sexual conduct

Victoria Gan also lost her sexual harassment case, but for a very different reason. Gan's work environment was crude and offensive. Her coworkers regularly spouted vulgarities and talked about sex. Once, they passed around a sex magazine and compared Gan's body to a woman in the magazine.

But Gan also used vulgarities, the court that heard her case noted in its opinion. She regularly talked about her sex life at work. She chose to sit with the men during lunch, even though other female employees avoided that area. Gan had once pinched the behind of a black coworker, and another time called him a "nigger." Since Gan didn't seem to mind the environment, the court judged that she could not have been harassed. The court concluded,

> [T]he working environment . . . was a very distasteful one, which, under different circumstances could certainly be conducive to sexual harassment charges. . . . [However,] the evidence shows that the allegedly harassing conduct was . . . welcomed and encouraged by plaintiff. She actively contributed to the distasteful working environment by her own profane and sexually suggestive conduct."[16]

In Victoria Gan's case, the court focused on an important word in sexual harassment law—the word *unwelcome*. From the first, sexual harassment had been described as unwelcome sexual conduct that interfered with work. If the conduct was not unwelcome, as the court ruled in Gan's case, then it was not harassment.

Like the phrase *severe or pervasive*, the word *unwelcome* played an important role in courtroom decisions during the 1980s. Many courts refused to judge sexual harassment cases by the harassing behavior alone. Sexual advances and crude remarks might or might not be harassment, the courts held. The determining factor was the unwelcomeness of the behavior.

Submitting to sexual demands

Although the legal focus on unwelcomeness undermined Victoria Gan's case, it would prove to be an important aid for many employees in their sexual harassment lawsuits. For women who had submitted to sexual demands, the emphasis on unwelcomeness was especially important. Unwelcomeness worked both ways. Welcome sexual advances and welcome crude remarks were not sexual harassment, the courts ruled. But unwelcome sexual advances and unwelcome crude remarks were sexual harassment.

For example, Mechelle Vinson almost lost her lawsuit when a court ignored the word *unwelcome* in its ruling. Vinson, a bank teller, had been propositioned by the vice president of her branch. Vinson submitted and had sex with him. Over the next three years, the vice president demanded sex from Vinson countless times.

Vinson's case represented one possible outcome of sexual harassment. Instead of rejecting her supervisor's sexual demands, Vinson had given in, only to find that having sex with her supervisor became a condition of work. In court, Vinson even testified that, when she refused to submit to the vice president on more than one occasion, he had forced himself on her. Further, he sometimes fondled her in front of other employees and had once followed her into the bathroom, exposing himself.

Vinson had faced unwelcome sexual conduct which created a hostile environment. However, the first court to hear Vinson's case was unsympathetic to her situation. The court replaced the stress on "unwelcome" sexual conduct

A woman who was sexually harassed describes her lawsuit against the perpetrator. Such lawsuits may be dismissed if the behavior is not found to be unwelcome.

with a stress on "voluntary" sexual conduct, ruling that Vinson could not claim harassment since she had "voluntar[ily]" had sex with her supervisor. Ignoring much of Vinson's testimony, the court ruled against her. Vinson and her lawyers appealed the case, and, in March 1986, their appeal reached the Supreme Court.

In an important decision, the Supreme Court ruled unanimously in Vinson's favor. The Supreme Court justices forcefully disagreed with the lower court's reasoning. Recognizing the power of the vice president to coerce Vinson into sex, they reminded the lower court that "unwelcome" was the issue in such a case, not "voluntary." Vinson's sex with the vice president was clearly unwelcome, the Court held. The unwelcomeness of the sex, plus the incidents of fondling and indecent exposure, had clearly turned Vinson's workplace into a hostile working environment.

The Court handed down its landmark decision in *Meritor Savings Bank v Vinson*. *Meritor* marked a critical moment in sexual harassment law. The high court affirmed many of the established criteria for judging sexual harassment lawsuits. It upheld both quid pro quo and hostile environment as valid legal claims. The Court ruled that severe or pervasive was the appropriate measure for hostile environment cases. Also, the Court decreed that "unwelcome" sexual conduct was sexual harassment.

The unanimous ruling in *Meritor* sent a clear message to lower courts. All nine Supreme Court justices, often at odds, agreed on the issue of sexual harassment. Expressing the opinion of the entire Court, Chief Justice William Rehnquist wrote, "Sexual harassment is . . . [an] arbitrary barrier to sexual equality at the workplace."[17]

Today's definition

Today, sexual harassment is defined as "unwelcome sexual conduct," including "unwelcome sexual advances, requests for sexual favors, and other verbal or physical conduct of a sexual nature."[18] Demeaning sexual graffiti and pornographic images at work are also considered, by many courts, a form of sexual intimidation.

Chief Justice William Rehnquist described sexual harassment as a barrier to equality.

Sexual harassment in the workplace is illegal when "submission to or rejection of such conduct by an individual is used as the basis for employment decisions affecting such individual," called quid pro quo harassment. Sexual harassment is also illegal when it "has the purpose or effect of unreasonably interfering with an individual's work performance or creating an intimidating, hostile, or offensive working environment," called hostile environment harassment.[19]

This definition is used by the Equal Employment Opportunity Commission, the government agency charged with enforcing laws against discrimination at work. In many ways, the government's definition reflects the early definitions of women's rights activists, women's magazines, and the experiences of women themselves at work.

2

Sexual Harassment in the Workplace

LAURA KOCH LEARNED about sexual harassment in the workplace when she took her first job, a summertime position before she went off to college. She worked at a Howard Johnson's motel answering phone calls. Her manager gave her a uniform that was too short and too tight for her. She did not have to buy a new uniform, he told her, since she was "only there for the summer." Koch found herself wearing a skirt so short that she could not bend over. Every night when Koch finished work, the assistant manager asked her for a hug. She remembers: "I'd hold my breath, tense myself and give the hug so I could go home." The assistant manager always patted her on the buttocks when he hugged her. Koch never complained about the behavior. Instead, she "counted the days until September" when she could leave.[20]

Susan Stegall also learned about sexual harassment on the job at an early age. "From the ninth grade until I graduated from college," she recalls, "I worked as either an aerobics instructor or a waitress." As an aerobics instructor, Stegall's boss regularly commented, "Are you turned on?" and, "I just love it that you all have to wear leotards and tights." As a waitress, businessmen regularly targeted her for sexual comments. "I wanted to work because I wanted to have my independence," Stegall explains. "But it seems like in every job, I ran into men being really gross." Ultimately, Stegall would find satisfying work at a family

23

violence unit, giving legal support to women who faced batterers at home. "I felt so much better about myself," she remarks, "because I wasn't being sexually harassed."[21]

Sexual harassment on the job is a common experience for many women in all types of workplaces. In a 1993 American Medical Association survey, 42 percent of female physicians reported experiencing sexual harassment while they practiced medicine. A 1989 *National Law Journal* survey revealed that 60 percent of female lawyers at top law firms have encountered sexual harassment. More than half of the women who responded to a 1991 poll by the National Association of Female Executives reported that they or someone they knew had been sexually harassed on the job. Further, countless women have described their own experiences of workplace sexual harassment in magazines, books, interviews, and studies.

This woman is one of the many who have reported experiencing sexual harassment on the job.

The Merit Systems survey

A comprehensive survey of workplace sexual harassment was released by the U.S. Merit Systems Protection Board in 1981. Merit Systems polled more than twenty thousand federal workers, and found that 42 percent of the female workforce —approximately two in five—had experienced sexual harassment on the job. Besides providing a general statistic, the Merit Systems survey offered a view into the types of harassment that were occurring in the federal workplace. Thirty-three percent of female workers reported being the target of unwelcome sexual remarks. More than one in four female workers reported pressure for dates. Fifteen percent reported unwelcome touching or cornering. One in eleven reported pressure for sexual favors. Further, one out of every hundred working women reported actual or attempted rape or assault in her workplace. *People Weekly* announced the Merit Systems survey with the headline,

"A Startling Study Claims That Sexual Harassment in the Office Is as Common as the Coffee Break."[22]

Sexual harassment leads to loss of employment and productivity

The American Medical Association survey, the *National Law Journal* survey, the National Association of Female Executives survey, and the Merit Systems survey, among others, have provided the type of comprehensive documentation necessary to show that sexual harassment is a problem in workplaces across the United States. This fact is important since it defines workplace harassment as a broad social issue. However, the simple existence of sexual harassment in the workplace has never been the central issue of workplace harassment. The central issue of sexual harassment on the job is the effect of sexual harassment on working women—and on the female workforce overall. Sexual harassment negatively affects the working women of the nation, and this is why sexual harassment has been taken up as a women's rights issue and an issue concerning the equality of the sexes.

The most obvious effect of workplace sexual harassment is the loss of employment. Many women have stories of jobs they left due to harassment. Janet Sassi left a weekly cleaning job because the man whose house she cleaned came up from behind her and fondled her breasts. Claudette Haynes left a waitressing job at a posh New York City restaurant because the cooks and waiters constantly made crude sexual comments and gestures, and one chef went so far as to expose his penis to her. A high-level manager at a Fortune 500 company, who identifies herself only as Claudia, left her managerial position because the vice president of her division treated her to vulgar sexual comments and repeatedly grabbed her and held her against her will.

How many women leave their jobs due to workplace sexual harassment? One of the first researchers to ask this question was psychologist Barbara Gutek in 1980. Gutek polled more than twelve hundred residents in the Los Angeles area and found that 10 percent of the women who

reported experiencing workplace sexual harassment had left their jobs because of their harassment.

One year later, in its survey of more than twenty thousand federal workers, the U.S. Merit Systems Protection Board arrived at an identical figure. Ten percent of sexually harassed federal employees reported quitting work because of sexual harassment. For Merit Systems, concerned with the federal workforce, this percentage translated into a staggering thirty thousand federal workers who could be expected to leave work because of harassment. Broadened to include working women in general, the same statistic meant the loss of employment for hundreds of thousands of women—at a conservative estimate.

When these statistics were released, the economic effect of sexual harassment on working women began to take shape. Sexual harassment in the workplace kept a portion of the female workforce moving from one job to the next. According to recent estimates, anywhere from 4 to 15 percent of sexually harassed working women lose their jobs because of their harassment.

Loss of employment is one important economic effect of sexual harassment on the job. Harassment also has a host of secondary effects on working women, including increased absenteeism and loss of productivity. Sometimes, for example, instead of quitting their jobs outright, women who experience sexual harassment on the job call in sick or use vacation time to avoid harassment. In one representative instance, a policewoman found herself calling in sick to avoid the constant sexual insults and pranks of her male counterparts. Ultimately, the policewoman was fired for taking off too much time from work.

Sexually harassed employees also waste valuable time when they avoid the people who harass them or cope with their harassment instead of working at the tasks on hand. For example, one woman reported that she could not use her company computers when she worked mornings because the man who harassed her typically used them during that time. Another described spending her first week at a new job learning how to avoid the sexual advances of her coworkers instead of learning her work duties. A third woman told of working late on a Friday night only to be rewarded with the unwelcome sexual advances of her supervisor.

In important early research conducted in 1978, absenteeism and loss of productivity as part of the effects of sexual harassment on employees has been documented. One woman in the study summarized the effects of workplace harassment in blunt language. "I hated to go to work," she explained.[23] Since that time, this research has been confirmed. Today, absenteeism and loss of productivity are a well-established part of the negative effect of sexual harassment on working women.

Sexual harassment keeps women away from male-dominated workplaces

Sexual harassment affects working women—and the female workforce overall—by leading to loss of employment, absenteeism, and loss of productivity. The economic effect of such behavior is clear. But sexual harassment has another important effect on working women. Harassment reduces the number of women applying for historically male-only positions.

Male-dominated fields, such as transportation and construction, are notorious as sites of sexual harassment. Examples of the most extreme harassment often occur when women work in an all-male environment. When Diane Joyce took a job on a road crew, her coworkers locked the women's bathroom on site, gave her faulty instructions for operating machinery, and scrawled obscene graffiti about Joyce around the workplace. When air traffic controller Deborah Katz worked in a male-dominated environment at a Virginia airport, she was regularly insulted with extreme sexual slurs and pressured for sex. When Donna Llewellyn worked with all-male coworkers as a truck driver, her coworkers formed a club to see who would be the first to have sex with her. Llewellyn was forced to quit after one of them burst in on her in the restroom and exposed himself to her. These women chose to work in jobs that are traditionally male, and they faced harassment because of this decision.

A female field technician works on a circuit box at the top of a telephone pole. Women in traditionally male-dominated fields experience higher rates of sexual harassment.

Research has confirmed that sexual harassment increases when more than 75 percent of the employees in a given workplace are male. All of the negative effects of sexual harassment—loss of employment, absenteeism, and loss of productivity—can therefore be expected to affect women who enter male-dominated workplaces more than women in female-dominated workplaces.

High-wage positions

At first glance, this fact may not appear to have a direct economic effect on working women. The economic effect becomes clear, however, when taken with another basic fact of employment: Jobs that are dominated by men often pay better than jobs that are dominated by women.

These types of jobs include high-wage blue-collar positions in trans-

Highly paid female construction workers are a rarity at most job sites.

portation, road work, and construction—traditional male work that pays better than the comparable food service, clerical, and child care jobs held mostly by women. However, these high-wage blue-collar jobs are not the only high-paid positions where few women can be found. According to a 1995 federal commission report, men also account for 95 to 97 percent of the senior managers among the top one thousand industrial firms and the five hundred largest firms of any type in the United States. Working women who reach high-level management positions can therefore also expect to encounter a significant level of sexual harassment. How much harassment occurs in these positions? Business consultant Freada Klein reports that approximately one in three female partners in private firms are sexually harassed during the course of a single year.

Sexual harassment, therefore, makes it more difficult for women to move into highly paid, male-dominated employment—no matter what the type of employment or associated income level. This effect has arguably the most significant negative economic impact of sexual harassment on working women and on the female workforce overall.

Economic losses provide a motivation for employers to stop harassment

With the negative effect of sexual harassment on the job firmly established, researchers and activists have turned toward calls for action to end sexual harassment. Focusing on employers, *Working Woman* magazine released a 1988 estimate for the approximate annual financial losses a company could expect if it did nothing to prevent sexual harassment in its workplace. "Sexual harassment costs a typical Fortune 500 company . . . $6.7 million per year in absenteeism, low productivity and employee turnover," *Working Woman* reported.[24] *Working Woman* hoped to motivate businesses by turning statistics about the economic effect of sexual harassment on working women into statistics on the financial cost of workplace harassment for the employer.

Economic losses provide one motivation for employers to take steps against sexual harassment in the workplace. However, other factors often lead companies to tolerate harassment, especially when harassment occurs between supervisor and subordinate. A company typically values a supervisor over a subordinate, since the supervisor holds a higher position within the business. A company may therefore be willing to see a lower-level female employee leave to preserve the position of a higher-level male employee, even if it means allowing sexual harassment to occur. For example, when ABC executive director Cecily Coleman filed a complaint within the company alleging that the vice president for corporate affairs had attempted to fondle her in his office and was pressuring her for sexual favors, ABC terminated Coleman instead of investigating the complaint against the vice president. Clearly, the vice president for corporate affairs was more important to the company than Coleman or the other women whom he may have harassed. "It's difficult to apply discipline even handedly," reports *Working Woman* correspondent Ronni Sandroff. "[I]t's always tougher to dismiss a high-ranking executive or a star performer."[25]

As demonstrated by ABC's response to Coleman's harassment complaint, an employer's response can have a real effect on sexual harassment in the workplace. ABC's response reportedly had a chilling effect on its other female employees. The type of retaliation that Coleman faced, however, is clearly an extreme response to a complaint of sexual harassment. A more typical employer response, but one that obtains no better results, is an indifferent dismissal of the situation. When an employer ignores sexual harassment in the workplace, the employer sends an implicit message to workers, and the harassment often grows worse.

For example, warehouse worker Carol Zabkowicz complained to her plant manager about the severe verbal harassment that she was enduring from several of her coworkers. The plant manager responded by reciting a few workplace rules to the coworkers, but took no disciplinary actions—not even informal ones. As a result, the coworkers' harassment of Zabkowicz intensified.

'No, my little sexpot, "harassment" has one r and two s's.'

Poor employer responses to reports of sexual harassment are common. A 1991 poll conducted by the National Association of Female Executives found that many of the working women who reported harassment within their company were ultimately forced out of the company, resigned, or were transferred to another position.

A positive employer response, on the other hand, can put a quick end to harassment on the job. For example, when International Telcom received a complaint that their vice president for sales had made an unwelcome sexual advance toward a subordinate, Telcom placed the vice president on warning, and, more importantly, required him to attend sessions with a sexual harassment counselor. The vice president attended the sessions on sexual harassment and respected what he learned during those sessions. The sexual harassment counselor who worked with the vice president reported, "In all probability, he is one of the vast majority of men who will never repeat their harassing behavior." [26]

Advice for companies

Business consultants offer standard advice for companies that are serious about stopping sexual harassment in the workplace. Top management at the company should write a strongly worded policy against sexual harassment, call one or several meetings to announce this policy, have clear instructions for filing formal sexual harassment grievances, assure employees that grievances will be taken seriously, and act quickly and responsibly when a grievance is actually brought forward. Naming one manager as an official sexual harassment ombudsman (helper) to answer questions and handle complaints is another recommended measure. Also, companies are urged to provide sexual harassment training for their employees.

When addressing the issue of sexual harassment within a company, management experts maintain, support from the top management of the company is critical. Harley-Davidson CEO Richard Teerlink, for example, held a concise ten-minute meeting with his top managers. Teerlink told them: "It's not just an issue of what's legal or illegal, but what's right and wrong and how do you treat people in the workplace. Managers will be held accountable for the environment your workers have to live in."[27] According to the director of Harley-Davidson's human resources department, Teerlink's brief and powerful message had a significant effect on the company. When company employees believe that the top managers are earnest in their efforts to end harassment, they typically support their superiors' policy against harassment.

Legal action may be an option

If an employee faces serious or repeated sexual harassment on the job and her employer does not act to stop the harassment, then the sexually harassed employee may have the option of bringing legal action against her employer.

Federal laws against sexual harassment on the job are based on Title VII of the Civil Rights Act of 1964, which makes it illegal for an employer to discriminate on the basis of sex. Since sexual harassment is, by definition, harassment that an employee encounters because of her sex, sexual harassment is considered to be a form of sex discrimination. However, Title VII of the Civil Rights Act of 1964 only applies to companies with fifteen or more employees. If a worker is sexually harassed at a company with fewer than fifteen employees, she does not qualify to bring a lawsuit under Title VII. Many states do have laws against sexual harassment that apply to smaller companies. If an employee lives in a state with these laws, she may be able to move forward with a sexual harassment lawsuit. If an employee lives in a state without these laws, however, and works at a business with fewer than fifteen employees, she has no legal remedies available to her under sexual harassment statutes.

Employees who file suits face obstacles

Sexually harassed employees who have the option to file a lawsuit will face a series of obstacles. First, filing a lawsuit costs money. In 1996, the average cost of retaining a lawyer for a case of sexual harassment ranged from $2,500 to $7,500. Low-income employees occasionally qualify for legal aid. Nevertheless, many employees with strong cases do not proceed with lawsuits because they cannot afford the expense.

If an employee has the money to move forward with a sexual harassment lawsuit, she will often find herself facing unsympathetic tactics from the employer's defense attorneys. Defense attorneys typically request the employee's medical and school records, and they interview coworkers, family, and friends in an effort to find damaging facts from the employee's past. As Lynn Hecht Schafran, Esq., from the NOW (National Organization for Women) Legal Defense and Education Fund explains,

> In litigation, every aspect of the plaintiff's life will be scrutinized [studied] . . . no matter how seemingly remote. [G]oing through it will be harrowing and will require support from every source the plaintiff can muster.[28]

Long delays are another problem with bringing legal action. Typically, the final verdict in a sexual harassment lawsuit is handed down years after the sexual harassment took place. In one extreme instance, Paula Jones, who filed a sexual harassment lawsuit against President Bill Clinton in 1994, spent years in litigation simply to proceed with her hearing. Jones's case against President Clinton centered on Clinton's alleged sexual advances toward Jones during his term as governor of Arkansas. The president's lawyers argued that a citizen should not have the right to sue an acting president and fought to delay Jones's trial until the year 2001, when President Clinton would step down from office. The Supreme Court, however, ruled that such a long delay could seriously damage Jones's case, since delays often result in the loss of important evidence, including "the inability of witnesses to recall specific facts."[29] The high court held that Jones's lawsuit should go forward. Nevertheless, by the time of the high court's ruling, the president's lawyers had already succeeded in delaying Jones's case for three years.

Jones's situation was unique. However, sexually harassed employees often wait one, two, or several years to enter the courtroom, making it more difficult for them to prove their cases.

For the ordinary working woman, filing a sexual harassment lawsuit is not a realistic option. The possibility of lawsuits, however, is seen as one motivating factor for employers to act responsibly when one of their employees is sexually harassed. This is especially true among companies that employ hundreds or thousands of employees. In these companies, there is a real possibility that an instance of serious or repeated sexual harassment could lead to a lawsuit if the company does not handle the situation properly. The Civil Rights Act of 1991 gave sexually harassed employees the right to receive as much as $300,000 in punitive damages. The costs of sexual harassment training within a company, even a large company, are often less than the cost of a single lawsuit.

A 1994 photo shows Paula Jones discussing her sexual harassment allegations against President Bill Clinton.

Equal Employment Opportunity Commission

The Equal Employment Opportunity Commission (EEOC) is the government agency charged with fighting all types of discrimination in the workplace, including sex discrimination. This is a tall order, and the commission has not always had full support from the Congress or the president. In the 1980s, the EEOC's budget was drastically reduced. From 1990 to 1995, while sexual harassment complaints more than doubled, the EEOC's budget was increased by a small 26 percent—approximately one-fourth. Currently, the EEOC has a backlog of more than seventy-four thousand cases. The commission simply cannot process the overwhelming number of discrimination complaints it receives. "The underfunded EEOC is struggling to stay on top of a heavy caseload," reports one *Business Week* correspondent. "For harassment victims, an EEOC overhaul can't come soon enough."[30]

Ideally, the EEOC is supposed to investigate complaints of sexual harassment, attempt to settle the complaints if it finds just cause, and take to court those that cannot be settled. In reality, many complainants file with the EEOC to receive a right-to-sue letter, which employees need to file a lawsuit, and then they continue their cases on their own. In 1995, the EEOC took sixty-six sexual harassment claims to court.

Class-action lawsuits

Since the EEOC can only take on a small number of lawsuits, the commission often brings a special type of action, called a class-action lawsuit. A class-action lawsuit includes a number of plaintiffs—those with complaints—against a single defendant. The EEOC tries to find cases where many women have been sexually harassed in one workplace and files on behalf of all the women. The commission then proves that a general pattern of sexual harassment occurred in the workplace. If it succeeds, the individual women can step forward and each receive an award, depending on the severity of her complaint. In a recent settlement, for example, the EEOC won $1.3 million for seventeen women who were all sexually harassed by a single office manager. The women will divide the settlement according to the severity of the harassment that each

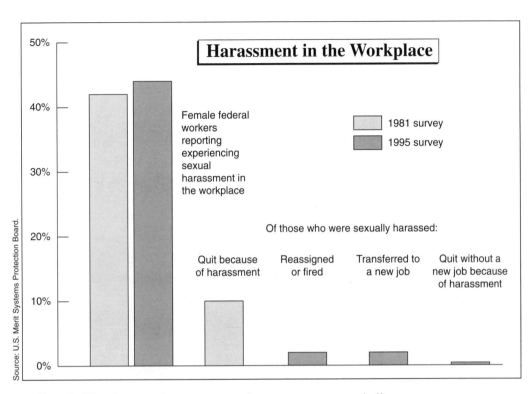

Harassment in the Workplace

Female federal workers reporting experiencing sexual harassment in the workplace

1981 survey
1995 survey

Of those who were sexually harassed:

Quit because of harassment | Reassigned or fired | Transferred to a new job | Quit without a new job because of harassment

Source: U.S. Merit Systems Protection Board.

suffered. "In class actions, we can impact more people," explains Cynthia Pierre, deputy director of the EEOC Chicago office.[31] For the most part, however, the EEOC can only hope to make headlines with high-profile cases and occasionally with a unique lawsuit that might in some way change the law.

Attention to sexual harassment in the workplace has made a difference

In 1995, the U.S. Merit Systems Protection Board released the findings of a new survey of sexual harassment in the federal workplace, fourteen years after the release of the original Merit Systems survey. According to the new statistics, approximately the same percentage of female federal workers report experiencing sexual harassment in the workplace—44 percent today compared with 42 percent in 1980.

However, according to the survey, the effect of sexual harassment on female federal workers has diminished. Of the female workers who experienced sexual harassment, 2 percent were reassigned or fired, 2 percent transferred to a new job, and one-tenth of 1 percent quit without a new job because of their harassment. These statistics are not heartening to the women who lost their jobs due to harassment. However, they do represent a decrease from earlier statistics. Policies against sexual harassment in the federal workplace and employee training are believed to account for a part of the reduced impact. More than three-quarters of the employees in the federal workplace reported attending training on the issues surrounding harassment. Sexual harassment has been taken seriously in the federal workplace, and it appears that these efforts have begun to make a difference.

Nevertheless, sexual harassment in the federal workplace from April 1992 though April 1994 cost taxpayers an estimated $327.1 million in employee turnover, absenteeism, and loss of productivity. The cost to female federal workers was even higher. An estimated 19,727 women were forced to leave their jobs because of harassment.

Sexual harassment in the workplace reinforces the economic inequalities between female and male workers. When women are fully represented at all levels of the economy, sexual harassment in the workplace is expected to abate. Until that time, employers are legally obligated to act when sexual harassment interferes with an employee's job performance or her ability to move ahead in her chosen vocation. Employers benefit from stopping sexual harassment in the workplace, but the true beneficiaries of employer action are the working women of the nation.

3

Sexual Harassment in Education

STUDENTS MIGHT BE sexually harassed in the classroom, in school corridors, or on a college campus. Just as serious or repeated sexual harassment is illegal in the workplace, so too is serious or repeated sexual harassment illegal in educational settings.

Laws against sexual harassment in education are based on Title IX of the Education Amendments of 1972, a law passed by Congress that makes it illegal for public schools to discriminate on the basis of sex. According to Title IX, public schools are required to offer equal educational opportunities for both sexes. The courts have interpreted Title IX to mean that both sexes must be treated equally at school. Public schools must therefore assure that students of one sex are not seriously or repeatedly sexually harassed. If students are harassed in such a manner, according to the law, they are being denied their right to an equal education.

In the courtroom, sexual harassment in education is measured by the same standards as sexual harassment in the workplace. Quid pro quo sexual harassment occurs in education when students are unfairly graded, denied recommendations, or denied equal access to classes because they reject the sexual advances of a teacher or administrator. For example, if a student says no to a teacher's sexual advances and the teacher gives her a bad grade, then she has faced quid pro quo sexual harassment. Hostile environment sexual harassment occurs in education when students

Schools are responsible for providing equal education for all students, including an environment free from sexual harassment.

face sexual harassment severe or pervasive enough either to affect their studies or to create an educational environment hostile to a member of their sex. Hostile environment sexual harassment includes unwelcome sexual touching, unwelcome sexual insults and slurs, unwelcome rumors about a student's sexual activity, unwelcome displays of pornographic images, unwelcome sexual advances, and any other unwelcome conduct that a student endures because of the student's sex.

There are exceptions, however, to the law. If a school does not receive any federal funding, then it does not have to abide by Title IX. Private secondary and elementary schools, therefore, do not always fall under the jurisdiction of federal laws against sexual harassment.

Private universities, on the other hand, almost always obtain money from the government through student loan programs and research grants, so they usually have to meet the requirements of Title IX. Thus, almost all colleges and universities are legally required to offer equal opportunities to students of both sexes, which includes the opportunity to attend school free from serious or repeated sexual harassment.

Sexual harassment in secondary school

According to surveys, sexual harassment is more common in secondary school than in any other setting. The most comprehensive survey of sexual harassment was conducted by the American Association of University Women (AAUW) in February and March of 1993. The AAUW polled sixteen hundred students, grades eight through eleven, chosen from seventy-nine schools nationwide. The results of their survey were so dramatic that the AAUW released the survey's findings under the title *Hostile Hallways*—a name that referred to the disturbing picture of widespread sexual harassment uncovered in the nation's schools.

In the AAUW poll, 89 percent of female students reported experiencing sexual harassment in school. Two out of three female students reported unwelcome sexual conduct "often" or "occasionally." Thirty-eight percent of female students reported being "blocked or cornered in a sexual way." One in four reported sexual harassment from

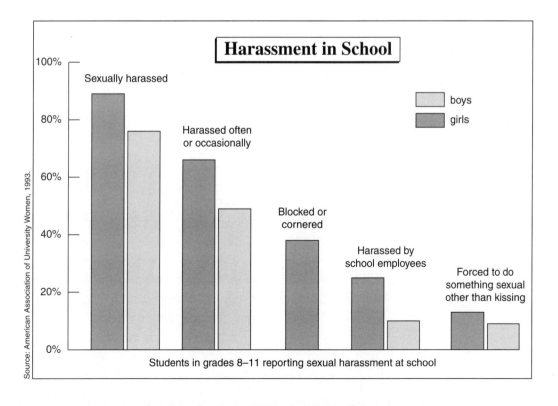

Harassment in School

Source: American Association of University Women, 1993.

Students in grades 8–11 reporting sexual harassment at school

school employees, including teachers, coaches, bus drivers, aides, security guards, principals, and counselors. Further, 13 percent of female students said they had been "forced to do something sexual at school other than kissing." Male students also reported unwelcome sexual conduct. Male students cited verbal harassment such as being called "gay" and having their "clothing pulled off or down." One in ten male students had been harassed by a school employee. One in eleven male students also reported being "forced to do something sexual at school other than kissing."[32]

What were the effects of sexual harassment on secondary school students? Sexually harassed students reported not wanting to attend school, not wanting to ask questions in class, feeling embarrassed and humiliated, scoring poorly on exams or in class grades, and fearing for their personal safety. At the very least, students who were sexually harassed at school had difficulty keeping their minds on their studies. At worst, these students were facing the devastating physical and psychological harm of real sexual abuse.

The AAUW called the survey results a "bleak picture." "The findings . . . confirm that sexual harassment is a major problem for many students," announced Alice McKee, president of the AAUW Educational Foundation, "one we can no longer afford to ignore."[33]

School officials ignore sexual harassment

Despite the AAUW findings, however, sexual harassment is a problem that schools often ignore. Sometimes, teachers, school staff, and school administrators allow sexual harassment to go on without a word. Other times, they try to stop the behavior, but without much effort. Either way, school officials often do not meet their legal obligations to assure that students can attend school without being seriously or repeatedly sexually harassed.

In one case, a middle school teacher regularly visited girls at a lunch table in the middle of a busy cafeteria. He ran his fingers up their thighs, grabbed them from behind

One poll reported that 89 percent of female students experienced sexual harassment at school. Such harassment compromises education and can cause psychological and physical harm.

to "tickle" them, touched their breasts, and looked down their shirts. Adults in the cafeteria did not call the teacher on his behavior, even though it was happening in public. The girls themselves had to speak out. Even then, the girls' complaints were dismissed by school officials. "At that time," the principal later stated, "I did not consider tickling to be sexual harassment." [34]

In another instance, an eighth-grade girl was seriously and repeatedly harassed by boys at school for an entire year. The boys shouted vulgar remarks about her body, pursued her in the hallway in groups, and intimidated her with sexual comments while she rode the bus. A lunchtime supervisor, a history teacher, and two assistant principals were witnesses to the harassment, but only the school's head custodian and one substitute teacher thought to go to the principal with a complaint. The principal's response was then disturbingly halfhearted. He attempted to put an end to the harassment but never bothered to check afterwards if it had stopped. When the girl's parents complained, the principal suggested that they try home schooling. The principal characterized the behavior as teasing.

These two cases represent typical responses to sexual harassment at school. Harassment is often dismissed as tickling, teasing, or with the phrase "boys will be boys."

Unfortunately, it is the students who lose from this inappropriate response.

To help schools respond more appropriately, the U.S. Department of Education Office for Civil Rights (OCR) recently published an easy-to-read pamphlet for school administrators. The OCR is the federal government agency charged with enforcing laws against sexual harassment in educational settings. In its pamphlet, the OCR offers specific advice for school officials who might ignore or downplay sexual harassment in their school:

> A school should not excuse . . . [sexual] harassment with an attitude of "that's just emerging adolescent sexuality" or "boys will be boys." This does nothing to stop the sexual harassment, and can even send a message that such conduct is accepted or tolerated by the school."[35]

Students have legal rights

When students are seriously or repeatedly sexually harassed at school, they have a legal right to demand that the harassment be stopped. If school officials do little or nothing to stop sexual harassment, then harassment can sometimes be stopped by students and their families acting on their legal rights.

Student Katy Lyle stands as an example of this fact. When Lyle was in ninth grade, boys at school wrote graffiti about her over an entire stall in the bathroom. "Katy Lyle is a slut," read a typical comment.[36] Encouraged by these words, the boys targeted her for verbal harassment in the hallways and on the bus to and from school, making constant remarks about her sex life, her body, and insulting her with vulgar sexual language. School officials did not intervene. When Lyle complained to the principal about the graffiti, he told her, "No one reads it anyhow," and "It'll make you a stronger person."[37] Lyle and her parents complained to the principal sixteen times but nothing was done.

In her tenth grade year, however, a year and a half since the harassment had begun, Lyle learned from an outsider that she could bring the weight of the law to bear upon the school. Lyle recalls this turn of events vividly: "I suddenly felt angry, feisty again. I called the school board and asked for an apology from the principal, as well as a letter explaining sexual harassment to students, and a new policy to teach the issue in local schools. And I filed a complaint with the Minnesota Human Rights Department."[38]

Suddenly, Lyle got action. With a district attorney on her side, the school agreed to her demands and paid $15,000 to compensate Lyle for two years of equal education denied.

Ideally, schools are supposed to inform students and parents of the students' right to an equal education. Many schools, however, simply have printed policies that do not get the message out. For example, schools in Katy Lyle's state of Minnesota were polled about their sexual harassment policies in 1993, several years after Lyle had settled her case, and only two out of every five schools believed that their students and staff understood the school's sexual harassment policy. The results were called "discouraging."

"Students are not informed about ways to avoid harassment and defend their rights," explain Susan Strauss and Pamela Espeland in their book *Sexual Harassment and Teens.*[39] In schools, where teachers and administrators typically have the last word, few students or parents realize that they can step outside of this system. When students and parents do not know their rights under the law, they often believe that a student has no choice but to live with sexual harassment at school, no matter how severe the harassment or how much it affects the student's grades and ability to learn. Getting the word out about the rights of students is an important part of eliminating sexual harassment in school. If school officials do not fulfill their legal obligations to stop serious or repeated sexual harassment, then students and parents may have to move beyond their school district. They can lodge a charge with the Office for Civil Rights in the Department of Education, with their state's department of education, or they can file a lawsuit on their own under Title IX.

Recommendations for secondary schools

Sexual harassment experts have worked hard to help school officials learn how to stop harassment in school.

Schools should inform students and parents of their legal rights, experts suggest. In addition, schools should explain the procedures for filing sexual harassment complaints, train all school staff to recognize and respond to sexual harassment, and integrate discussions of sexual harassment into their curriculum. "No singular approach can eliminate and prevent sexual harassment in schools," experts Nan Stein and Lisa Sjostrom explain in *Flirting or Hurting?* their 1994 sexual harassment curriculum resource.[40] Stein and Sjostrom point out that the problem of sexual harassment in school needs to be addressed in many ways.

Besides solutions that involve the adults in a school, Stein and Sjostrom recommend that students work as activists. Students should request time on the agenda of faculty and school board meetings to bring the problem of sexual harassment to the school's attention, they suggest, and students can also write articles on sexual harassment for the school newspaper. Stein and Sjostrom further believe that students should learn to speak out when they see sexual harassment happening in their school. "If you . . . see someone being harassed, speak up!" they suggest. "Offer your support to the target—whether you know the person or not."[41] Sexual harassment in schools can clearly be

Students can help stop sexual harassment by speaking up when they witness harassment.

reduced if students make the personal decision to stop harassment when they see it.

Nonetheless, schools should not expect students to bear the burden and responsibility of stopping harassment, Stein and Sjostrom explain. Teachers and staff are expected to be the first to act when sexual harassment occurs. Stein maintains,

> Students have a right to expect that if something frightening, unpleasant or illegal is happening at school—especially if it is occurring in public—someone in authority will intervene to stop it. The silence of adults clearly represents negligence, allowing and encouraging the harassment to continue.[42]

Sexual harassment in elementary school

In the fall of 1996, news reports placed an interesting issue before the American public. At least a couple of elementary schools, it seemed, were misusing their sexual harassment policies to discipline children who had not engaged in sexual harassment. The first such incident occurred in Lexington, North Carolina, where six-year-old Jonathan Prevette had been punished under his elementary school's sexual harassment policy. Prevette had kissed a girl in his class. When the girl complained, he was separated from the class for an entire day, left to color in another room while the other children had an ice-cream party.

Prevette went home and informed his parents that he was in "trouble." Prevette's mother called the school and was told by the principal that her son had "violated the sexual harassment policy" of the school. Prevette's mother described to a reporter what happened when she went to talk to the principal in person: "She gave me the sexual harassment policy, and proceeded to tell Jonathan what he did was wrong. If he was caught again kissing, hugging or hand-holding, he would be suspended."[43]

One week later, a similar incident occurred in Queens, New York. At Public School 104, seven-year-old De'Andre Dearinge was suspended for five days after kissing a girl and tearing a button from her skirt. Dearinge was sent home with a note, signed by the principal, stating that the boy was suspended for "sexual harassment."

48

"If you send me a Valentine's Day card, I'll have you busted for sexual harassment like that kid in North Carolina!"

Through media reports, it became clear to the American public that neither of these schools understood the meaning of sexual harassment. Lawyer Verna Williams, from the National Women's Law Center, explained succinctly why these kisses were not sexual harassment. Sexual harassment "doesn't reach a little boy kissing a girl," she stated. "That's not pervasive harassment, it's not a pattern, it's not severe, and sometimes a kiss is just a kiss."[44]

Child development experts agreed. The boys' unwelcome kisses might have been misbehavior, at most, a form of bullying. The teachers should have sat down with the boys, discussed the need to respect other students, and left it at that. Reporting the behavior as sexual harassment was a mistake in judgment, which demonstrated that the schools did not fully understand the issues involved in real harassment. Further, the schools' quick responses of suspension and separation from the class seemed problematic, regardless of the boys' behavior. "Using punitive measures . . . is not the way we should do this," explained Harvard professor T. Berry Brazelton.[45]

To correct the misunderstandings of the two "kissing boy" incidents, the OCR issued a statement clarifying its stance on the behavior of very young children. School officials can rely "entirely on their own judgment," the OCR pointed out, as long as misbehavior does not meet the legal standards of severe or pervasive. Schools are not under legal obligation to document minor behavior problems. In these cases, the OCR explained, schools may wish to use "more age-appropriate" methods to resolve conflicts between students.[46]

The two "kissing boy" incidents received an incredible amount of attention from the media, so much so that sexual harassment experts began to worry that the public might mistakenly believe that sexual harassment in elementary school was never a serious issue. Several magazines and newspapers, including *People Weekly*, the *Nation*, and the *Washington Post*, published articles expressing serious concern that the facts surrounding sexual harassment in

Steve Kelley/Copley News Service. Reprinted with permission.

schools would be lost amid the highly publicized "kissing boy" cases. As these articles pointed out, serious sexual harassment can and does occur in elementary schools, although much of the public may not be aware of it.

For example, in one case, a six-year-old girl became the target of harassment on the school bus to and from school. Older boys constantly taunted her with sexual slurs and sexual innuendoes. The girl's mother described the boys' vulgarities as the "foulest, most vulgar, obscene language I could ever imagine, that I hadn't heard till I was twenty years old."[47] An OCR investigation concluded that there was "no question" that the girl was sexually harassed and that "the [school] district knew or should have known of the occurrence of harassment but did not respond forcefully to end it."[48] In another case, elementary school boys were regularly allowed to spit on girls, shout obscenities, grab at girls' bodies, push girls to the ground, kiss girls, pinch girls' behinds, and hold girls in choke holds. Once again, the school was found at fault for ignoring the behavior.

Although it is possible for elementary schools to misuse their sexual harassment policies to punish children inappropriately, as in the two "kissing boy" incidents, it is clearly much more common for elementary schools not to use their sexual harassment policies even when they are required to do so by law.

Sexual harassment on campus

Colleges and universities have also struggled to meet the standards required by sexual harassment laws. Peer harassment is common on campus, especially in groups. Male students stand in front of fraternity houses shouting remarks at female students who walk by. Male students in cafeterias rate female students for sexual attributes. Graffiti in campus dorms and hallways can include violent images of women as well as derogatory statements. Female students who bring up women's issues in the classroom are sometimes booed, ridiculed, or shouted down by male students.

Students also encounter sexual harassment from professors. The issue of professor-student sexual harassment was first raised as early as 1977. In that year, a Connecticut district court ruled that quid pro quo sexual harassment was unlawful in a university setting, whenever a professor attempted to trade grades for sexual favors. Subsequently, research into sexual harassment revealed that this type of quid pro quo harassment was disturbingly common. In 1988, a survey of two thousand undergraduate and graduate students found that 9 percent of them had been directly propositioned by a professor, and 5 percent had experienced subtle or overt bribery for sexual favors. Research also revealed that female students regularly faced hostile environment sexual harassment from professors, including unwelcome sexual touching, sexual innuendo, sexual slurs, and hostility or insults directed at female students. Considering quid pro quo and hostile environment harassment together, surveys found that approximately 20 to 30 percent of undergraduate students experienced sexual harassment from professors, as did 30 to 40 percent of graduate students.

Repercussions and recommendations

What were the effects of professor-student sexual harassment on campus? Besides the expected embarrassment, frustration, and anxiety associated with being harassed by a professor, researchers found that female students were making decisions that affected their academic careers based on the sexually harassing conduct of their professors. Approximately one in five female graduate students reported skipping a class to avoid sexual harassment, and, in one survey, 13 percent of female students said they avoided a course or study with specific professors due to expected pressure for dates. Sexually harassed students also explained that they did not visit harassing professors during office hours even if they needed help in the class because they did not wish to be further targeted for harassment. Students further stated that they stopped asking these professors questions either in class or after class. Through these reports, it became clear to researchers that the sexual harassment of students by professors was having an overall negative effect on the education of female students.

Prevention of sexual harsassment on college and university campuses requires strong, clearly worded policies.

Sexual harassment experts crafted a series of recommendations for universities addressing the problem of sexual harassment on campus. These experts explained that universities needed to draft strong policies against sexual harassment and outline official grievance procedures for students to follow if they are being sexually harassed by one of their professors. Experts also recommended sexual harassment training for professors, university officials, and students. Further, universities were urged to name a specific individual or individuals on campus as a contact for students who were being sexually harassed.

Throughout the 1980s and into the 1990s, many colleges and universities have implemented these recommendations, motivated by legal rulings that held these institutions responsible for the sexual harassment. By 1997, according to Bernice Resnick Sandler, an expert on sex discrimination in higher education, most institutions of higher education were in "the 'second stage' of policy development . . . refining or 'fine tuning' their policy in light of their experiences with it."[49]

Academic freedom

Universities must take extra care when drafting and enforcing their policies against professor-student sexual harassment, however, because of a unique rule to which these institutions must adhere. The speech of professors in the classroom has traditionally been afforded special protection by the courts, based on the First Amendment's right to free speech. When enforcing policies against sexual harassment, universities have to assure that they do not discipline a professor for speech that is protected by law.

What type of classroom speech is protected by the First Amendment? The Supreme Court has not ruled on the scope of a public university professor's protected speech. However, it is generally accepted that a professor's classroom comments are protected by the First Amendment if the comments are relevant to the subject matter of the class. "Faculty members can . . . legitimately claim the protections afforded by the notion of academic freedom when they are functioning in their roles as educators and scholars," explain education professor Susan J. Scollay and law professor Carolyn S. Bratt in a discussion of academic freedom and sexual harassment.[50]

If a professor's classroom comments fall under the protection of the First Amendment, then, according to most accounts, the university cannot discipline the professor under its sexual harassment policy, even if his comments are repeated or serious enough to create a hostile environment to students of one sex. The Office of Civil Rights (OCR) in the Department of Education explains,

> [I]n responding to harassment that is sufficiently severe, persistent, or pervasive as to create a hostile environment . . . a school must formulate, interpret, and apply its rules so as to protect academic freedom and free speech rights. Academic discourse . . . is protected by the First Amendment even if it is offensive to individuals.[51]

Thus, the civil rights of students to an equal opportunity education regardless of their sex is generally interpreted to be less important than the rights of professors to academic freedom. Where a professor's free speech rights begin, it presently appears that laws against sexual harassment end—without exception.

Nevertheless, even though colleges and universities are constrained by the special legal protection afforded to a professor's classroom speech, there is a broad range of classroom speech that does not fall under the protection of the First Amendment. For example, a professor does not have the right to threaten students in the classroom, nor to single out a specific student for harassment or insults. Neither does a professor have the right to make comments that disrupt the educational environment of the classroom. Further, institutions of higher education are allowed to set the curriculum of a course, deciding the topics that a professor must cover during the semester. Also, a college or university is legally allowed to discipline a professor for remarks unrelated to the subject matter of the course. For example, the law does not protect a mathematics professor who insists on making repeated remarks that demean women while in the classroom.

Professors cannot spend their classroom lecture, therefore, arbitrarily making comments that demean one sex, referring to students with sexual slurs, leering at students, touching students in a sexual manner, or singling out students for insulting remarks or for remarks about their bodies. Colleges and universities are well within their rights to discipline a professor who creates a hostile environment in the classroom through these forms of speech, and, in fact, they are legally obligated to do so. It would appear that most classroom sexual harassment can be stopped without reference to speech protected by the legal interpretation of academic freedom.

However, at least a couple of institutions of higher education have run into problems disciplining professors for sexual harassment because of the academic freedom exemption that professors can claim. In one case, a court ruled that the discipline imposed on a professor for sexually harassing his female students had to be thrown out because some of the complaints against the professor involved sexual comments he made in the classroom—

A professor's lecture may not be subject to sexual harassment policies if the comments are relevant to the subject matter of the class.

comments the court believed were legitimately related to the material the professor was teaching. Even though several of the complaints against the professor involved comments directed at specific students outside of the classroom, the court held that "but for [the professor's] classroom statements he would not have been subject to . . . discipline."[52] The university was subsequently forced to drop all of its disciplinary actions against the professor.

Colleges and universities will, therefore, have to tread carefully when investigating a professor whose sexually harassing behavior includes sexual innuendoes in the classroom. Sexual harassment experts hope that, in the future, a clear line can be drawn between classroom speech that has legitimate ties to educational goals and classroom speech that has no legitimate ties to educational goals. Many also hope that the civil rights of students to receive an equal education will be given more weight in judicial decisions when free speech is at issue. Explains social psychology professor Linda Vaden Gratch,

> [T]he idea of uncensored voice is indeed essential to the process of discovery and teaching. It means that the professor and the student have the freedom to express their thoughts and beliefs. However, if through that free expression a whole class of people is intimidated and feels robbed of its opportunity to learn and participate in the educational system, the whole point of the activity of education is lost.[53]

Schools that receive money from the government are obligated by law to serve students of both sexes equally. This means that schools must provide an educational environment free from serious or repeated sexual harassment. Today, schools have yet to meet fully the challenges of providing an equal education for all students. Sexual harassment is still a part of everyday experience for the vast majority of female students. Schools must therefore keep the issue of sexual harassment in focus if they are going to fulfill the high ideal of equality in education.

4

Sexual Harassment in the Military

ON NOVEMBER 7, 1996, Secretary of the Army Togo D. West Jr. and Army Chief of Staff General Dennis J. Reimer publicly denounced sexual harassment in the army:

> [S]exual harassment is totally abhorrent to Army traditions and American values. The Army bases its success on mission accomplishment. Successful mission accomplishment can only be achieved in an environment of mutual respect, dignity, and fair treatment. This necessitates zero tolerance of sexual harassment.[54]

This declaration was issued in reaction to explosive news reports of sexual abuse, sexual harassment, and rape at the Aberdeen Proving Ground, an army training facility in Maryland. Officers entrusted with the mid-level training of recruits were forcing themselves on female recruits at Aberdeen, using the power of their rank as protection. By the time West and Reimer made their statement, three officers faced courts-martial for criminal conduct. Ultimately, twelve soldiers would stand accused.

Following the first reports of sexual abuse at Aberdeen, the army initiated a sexual harassment hot line, and thousands of complaints poured in. By November 17, the hot line had received more than four thousand calls, and by the end of December more than five thousand, at least eight hundred of which merited investigation. Through newspaper reports and televised interviews, it was becoming clear to Americans that the army had a serious problem with sexual harassment.

Army Chief of Staff Dennis Reimer (right) and Secretary of the Army Togo West Jr. discuss a report citing the prevalence of sexual harassment in the army.

But for women in the army, this was old news. When six female soldiers appeared on public television's *Lehrer News Hour*, there was a general consensus. "I know I wasn't surprised at all," Lieutenant Deborah Crew commented, referring to the events at Aberdeen. "I was disturbed by it, but I was not surprised." The other soldiers nodded their heads in agreement. Staff Sergeant Vanessa Whittington remarked, "Sexual harassment, you mean? I'm sure it takes place every day."[55]

A decrease in army sexual harassment

In stark contrast to these admissions, Secretary of the Army Togo West Jr. was shocked by the overwhelming number of complaints pouring in on the new army hot line. "It is the worst we have seen," he said in a CBS interview, "and we never expected it."[56] West may well have been surprised to hear of the widespread sexual harassment occurring in the army, but his surprise exposed a serious flaw in the way information about sexual harassment was being interpreted by officials at the top of command.

Only four months before the incidents at Aberdeen, the Department of Defense had released the findings of an impressively exhaustive survey on sexual harassment in the U.S. military. Over twenty-eight thousand active-duty military members had filled out questionnaires with detailed queries. The survey results, released July 2, 1996, included a wealth of important—and alarming—details on sexual harassment in the military. Fifty-two percent of the women in the military reported being sexually harassed within a twelve-month period. Thirteen percent had been sexually coerced. Six percent had been sexually assaulted, which included rape.

The task force that analyzed these results, however, came to a remarkable conclusion. "These survey results are encouraging," the task force decided. The task force pointed out that the results documented "a decline in harassment experiences," which was true.[57] Eight years earlier, a previous survey had shown that 64 percent of military women—more than three in five—had been sexually harassed. The new survey showed that number had dropped to between 52 to 55 percent, slightly over half. Almost immediately, a news release from the Department of Defense accepted this positive view of the survey's findings. "Sexual harassment in the active-duty military is declining," the Department of Defense announced.[58]

Secretary West discusses a Department of Defense survey that reported a drop in sexual harassment.

But converting the percentage into actual numbers meant that more than ninety-five thousand military women were being sexually harassed every year. Military officials saw only the statistical decline in harassment from 1988 to 1995. Officials looked at the numbers, but they did not attach these numbers to the lives of actual soldiers.

This view may have explained Secretary West's surprise at the outpouring of sexual harassment complaints. In a television interview after the events at Aberdeen had been released, West echoed the task force by stressing the positive elements of the Department of Defense survey. For many of those concerned with women's rights, however, a decrease in reports of sexual harassment from three-fifths of the women in the service to half of the women in the service over an eight-year period was not a very good record.

A failure in command

The events uncovered in 1996 at the Aberdeen Proving Ground were not the first reports of sexual harassment in the military. In 1992, a disturbing picture of sexual harassment in the navy emerged from media reports of the navy's annual Tailhook convention. The Tailhook convention was a traditional gathering of navy and marine pilots that took place every year in Las Vegas, Nevada. In 1991, the Tailhook convention had included lectures, speeches, and panel discussions. Salesmen visited from defense contractors such as McDonnell Douglas and Hughes. Top brass from the navy attended.

During the night, however, as an investigation would later reveal, navy and marine officers participated in wild parties, and they assaulted women who came to the parties. Reports of the officers' behavior shocked the American public. On the third floor of the Las Vegas Hilton, officers had lined the hallway, forcing women to walk between them while they clutched at the women and tore at the women's clothing. The officers called this "running the gauntlet."

According to later testimony, two officers had tried to put a stop to the assaults. These two officers had waited for a time at the front of the "gauntlet" line and warned women what would happen to them if they tried to walk down the hallway. Several women were able to leave before they were assaulted. The two officers, however, were ultimately pushed out by one of the aviators involved in the assaults. One of these officers explained:

> [The aviator] said the gauntlet was a Tailhook tradition and we were going against tradition. We tried to talk to him and confronted him about violating the women. He said the women knew what they were in for when they came to Tailhook.[59]

Sometime that night, Lieutenant Paula Coughlin would arrive on the third floor. She had no idea what was going on there. When the men started assaulting her, she punched them, kicked them, and bit one on the arm. "I thought, I have no control over these guys. I'm going to be gang-raped," Lieutenant Coughlin would later explain.[60] At least fourteen female officers as well as twelve civilian women were sexually assaulted during the convention.

Lieutenant Coughlin filed an official complaint and, when the results of the navy's investigation first came in, Secretary of the Navy H. Lawrence Garrett III took a position of outrage. He condemned the navy officers involved and declared that the navy would "not condone sexual harassment in any form, or tolerate those who permit it to exist."[61] Specifically, he noted, those who held leadership roles would be held responsible. However, a supplemental report to the investigation released shortly afterwards placed Secretary Garrett himself at the parties. Garrett was forced to admit this fact, although he stated that he had personally seen nothing "inappropriate or offensive." Shortly afterwards, Secretary Garrett resigned his post.

As the public would learn, many of the navy's admirals had attended the Tailhook parties. Admiral Jack Snyder was there. He was also the first admiral to hear Coughlin's complaints of sexual assault. Snyder's initial response to Coughlin's ordeal was clearly inappropriate. "That's what you've got to expect on the third deck with a bunch of

BY MARLETTE FOR NEWSDAY

"THIS ONE'S FOR *DESERT STORM*... THIS ONE'S FOR *BOSNIA*... AND THIS ONE'S FOR FIGHTING OFF MY *COMMANDING OFFICER!*"

drunk aviators," he had told her.[62] Admiral Snyder was quickly relieved of command. Three other admirals were issued letters of censure, and twenty-eight more admirals received nonpunitive letters of caution, as did one marine general. Ultimately, Admiral Frank Kelso, chief of naval operations, was forced to retire. Kelso, had testified that he was not present on the Hilton patio during the parties. However, in direct contradiction to this statement, the testimony of other officials placed him there.

Those who were found culpable, however, were not the only ones to be affected by the Tailhook sexual assaults. The first military woman to step forward with a complaint, Lieutenant Paula Coughlin, resigned in 1994, citing the hostility that she had faced since speaking out against the sexual assault.

Sexual harassment goes unreported

For Patrick B. Pexton, managing editor at Army Times Publishing Company, the sexual harassment at the navy Tailhook convention and on the army's Aberdeen training facility demonstrate a failure of the military's top leadership. Pexton notes a disturbing pattern in the conduct of top officials:

> The solution is an abrupt public declaration by generals or admirals that the misconduct will not be tolerated in any form. Conveniently forgotten are the leadership failures that led to the embarrassment in the first place.[63]

Like Pexton, many female soldiers have little faith in the top brass of their services when it comes to sexual harassment. In 1994, only 53 percent of military women stated that the top leadership was making "honest and reasonable attempts to stop sexual harassment."[64]

This lack of trust affects the resolution of sexual harassment incidents among soldiers. According to the 1995 Department of Defense sexual harassment survey, most of the sexual harassment in the military goes unreported, an estimated 60 percent of all incidents. Twenty percent of those who did not report the harassment remained silent because they felt that nothing would be done. Others felt that they would be labeled troublemakers or would be disbelieved.

An examination of reported sexual harassment complaints in the survey demonstrated that these concerns were well-founded. Nearly one-fourth of the military women who complained reported that their complaint was "not taken seriously." One out of every five complainants believed that their performance rating was "unfairly lowered" because they had spoken out.

The exclusion of women

Recommendations on how to remedy sexual harassment in the military often focus on structural changes. Retired air force lieutenant colonel Karen Johnson, currently a vice president of the National Organization for Women, believes that sexual harassment complaints should not be handled within the military's normal chain of command. Johnson has called for a separate Department of Defense team to handle complaints, so that military women can complain without fear of retaliation from their commanders. The armed forces cannot be trusted to investigate complaints against its own commanders, maintains Johnson. Military women need another avenue for complaints.

Another common recommendation is the inclusion of women into all combat positions. Currently, certain military positions including ground combat positions, special operations assignments, and submarine duty are not open to female personnel. Lieutenant Deborah Crew explains how the exclusion of women can increase sexual harassment in the military:

> I think there are some males who . . . maybe their vision of the army doesn't include women and so . . . if it doesn't include women, you can discriminate against them, you can harass them, you can do whatever it takes, because . . . they shouldn't be there anyway.[65]

Journalist and author Jean Zimmerman agrees with this assessment of harassment in the military. Zimmerman cites a telling incident from the 1991 Tailhook convention. During a daytime "Flag Panel" question-and-answer period with navy admirals, one female pilot asked about the future of women in navy aviation. The pilot's question was shouted down by the male officers. Zimmerman reports that Vice Admiral Richard Dunleavy answered the question, "[b]ut no one really heard him underneath the 'Woo-woo!' of the crowd."[66] This disrespect for military women during official events at Tailhook transformed into the sexual assaults on women by the same officers during the nighttime parties, Zimmerman believes. The disrespect for military women, she maintains, is fueled by their exclusion from prestigious military positions:

> What has been established in the aftermath of Tailhook is . . . the crucial relationship between respect and responsibility. Giving American women the right to prove themselves as warfighters establishes them on a new footing, as fully partic ipatory, first-class citizens.[67]

Republican senator Olympia Snowe of Maine also named the exclusion of women as a cause of sexual harassment in a 1997 television interview. "[W]omen should have the opportunity to enter higher . . . positions within the military," she declared. Sexual harassment in the military will stop,

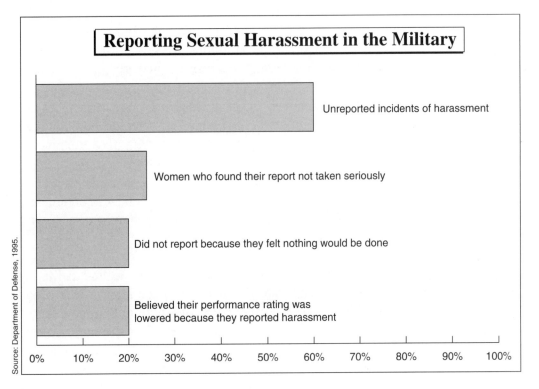

Source: Department of Defense, 1995.

Senator Snowe argued, when women are part of the highest echelons of military command. She stated flatly, "[I]t's important to have women . . . making the decisions."[68]

Women in combat

Combat exclusion depends on laws passed by Congress, which were for the most part repealed in 1991 and 1993. Ground combat positions, however, are still closed to women, an exclusion which has a clear effect in the army and the marines, where approximately one-third of positions are male only. Despite calls for the inclusion of women into ground combat positions, the army and marines have not embraced inclusion as a solution to sexual harassment. Since 1991, on the other hand, the navy and air force have opened almost all of their combat positions to women. The 1995 Department of Defense survey revealed that the incidences of sexual harassment in the navy and the air force, although alarmingly high, are measurably less than the incidences of sexual harassment in the army and the marines.

Some people, however, oppose the calls for greater inclusion of women into the military services because they believe that the inclusion of women will reduce the effectiveness of military units in combat. "We . . . need to do something about recruiting quotas that are increasing numbers of women," explains Elaine Donnelly, president of the public policy group Center for Military Readiness (CMR).[69] CMR maintains that female soldiers are "known to be less strong, less versatile, less deployable, and less likely to remain in the Army."[70] Mission effectiveness, CMR contends, must always be placed before what CMR sees as politically driven policies for recruiting women.

CMR is not alone in its opinion. In response to the sexual harassment at the Aberdeen Proving Ground, a *Washington Post* editorial voiced a similar sentiment. "In sorting out these issues, national security, not equal opportunity, should come first," the *Post* insisted. "The military's job is to defend the country and its interests. Women should be integrated only so far as they can help that mission."[71]

Jeanne Holm receives her stars for brigadier general in 1971. Holm was the first woman in the U.S. Air Force to attain this rank.

Many military officials firmly believe, however, that the military benefits from an increased number of women in its ranks. "The principal objective [of recruiting women] was to meet the overall manpower needs of the military," explains retired major general Jeanne Holm, who served on the Defense Advisory Committee on Women in the Services.[72] According to Major General Holm, the military has faced a shortage of recruits since it became an All-Volunteer Force in 1973. "In reality, by the late 1970s women were literally keeping the All-Volunteer Force afloat," she states. "[T]he trade-off was between low-quality men and high-quality women."[73]

Other top military officials agree with Holm. One senior defense official stated,

> Frankly, the expansion of opportunities for women in the military is based on the contribution they have made to the quality and readiness of our forces. . . . Thirty-five thousand women served in the Persian Gulf. Their performance was crucial to success.[74]

Separate training for women and men

To reduce sexual harassment in the military, certain congressional Republicans, among others, have argued that

A drill instructor trains female marine recruits to march in formation. The U.S. Marine Corps trains men and women separately in an effort to decrease sexual harassment.

the services should separate female soldiers from male soldiers in training, an option currently chosen only by the U.S. Marine Corps. Sexual harassment will decrease, they maintain, if women and men train separately when they first enter the services. During training, it is believed, recruits are more vulnerable to harassment. Expressing a representative opinion, Congressman Robert L. Livingston of Louisiana made this argument in a letter to the New Orleans *Times-Picayune:* "The facts indicate that the complete integration of men and women in all aspects of military life has proven to be a disaster." [75]

U.S. Army, Navy, and Air Force officials do not believe, however, that separating women from men during training is a viable option. A senior navy official explained the navy's training policy in a June 3, 1997, news briefing. "[W]e train the way we operate," he pointed out. "We train for operational combat units." Since women and men must work together during operation, he explained, the navy places them together for training. "[A]t the end of nine weeks we're sending them to an operational fleet that needs them trained and ready," he remarked. [76]

The army takes a similar stance. If army duties include women and men, officials believe, then they must train women and men together to complete these duties.

The military's response

Military officials have not endorsed structural changes in response to the acknowledged problems of sexual harassment within the military. They do not believe that a complaint system outside of the chain of command is the answer, as recommended by the National Organization for Women. Nor does it seem likely that the army and marines will call for the inclusion of women into ground combat positions, or that Congress will require this inclusion. On the other hand, the military continues to recruit women— an estimated 21 percent of army recruits are now women. The military finds that women recruits are highly qualified and believes that female soldiers strengthen military readiness and effectiveness. Neither does the military consider it realistic to train women and men separately for duties that they will perform together.

Instead, military officials believe that more training is the answer. On September 11, 1997, the army announced that it had decided to increase basic training by one week to strengthen its training on sexual harassment, which is incorporated into the basic values segment of basic training. The army also plans to alter its enforcement policy for violations of its code against sexual misconduct and screen its instructors more rigorously. Drill sergeants in charge of training recruits will be subjected to a psychological evaluation and a criminal background check. "The army's actions make it clear that there is no room for sexual abuse, harassment or discrimination in today's military," declared a September 1997 Department of Defense press release.[77]

At the same time, a panel of investigators led by a retired two-star general turned in its evaluation of the army's handling of sexual harassment. "We are firmly convinced that leadership is the fundamental issue," the panel's report concluded. "Passive leadership has allowed sexual harassment to persist."[78]

5

What About Men?

IN A RECENT study on the sexual harassment of men, one public utility worker expressed his experience: "I have never been harassed. Sexual harassment of men is hardly heard of in my job. I can't . . . recall of even hearing of sexual harassment towards men."[79]

Other men in the survey were even more forthcoming, stating that they were "not sexually harassed often enough," or, in one comment, that sexual harassment "kind of makes the job more fun."[80]

Research on sexual harassment has revealed what many suspected—sexual harassment is not a serious problem for most men. Men are not typically affected by comments about their bodies. They do not often mind pressure for dates. Also, men rarely find themselves on the wrong end of aggressive sexual conduct. Nevertheless, the sexual harassment of men does occur—more often than most researchers at first believed. The sexual harassment of men was first revealed in 1981, when the U.S. Merit Systems Protection Board released the results of its comprehensive sexual harassment survey. Merit Systems polled more than twenty thousand federal workers and found that 15 percent of the men reported experiencing sexual harassment. The chairwoman of Merit Systems, Ruth Prokop, called the results on male harassment "surprising."

Since that time, the findings of the Merit Systems survey have been confirmed. Approximately 14 to 17 percent of men in the workplace experience unwelcome sexual conduct. Twelve percent of male university professors report harassment, as do 14 percent of male military personnel.

In schools, male harassment is even more common. In 1993, when the American Association of University Women conducted an extensive survey of sexual harassment in secondary schools, they found that 76 percent of the male students had experienced sexual harassment at least once, and 49 percent had been sexually harassed "often" or "occasionally." Repeating Ruth Prokop's comment of twelve years previous, the AAUW called this high incidence of male sexual harassment "surprising."

The effect of sexual harassment on males

The AAUW examined its 1993 survey closely and discovered a critical difference between sexually harassed boys and sexually harassed girls. The sexually harassed boys did not experience the same drastic effects as the sexually harassed girls. Almost one in four girls had seen their grades suffer because of sexual harassment, but only one in

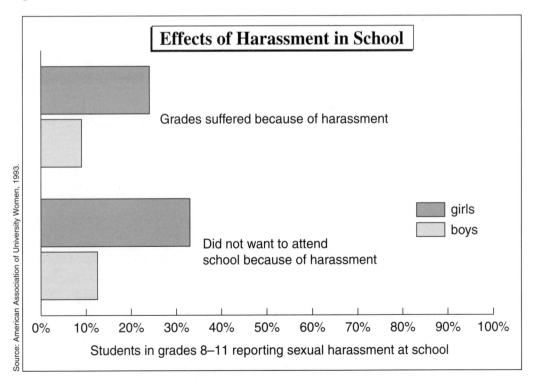

eleven boys reported the same decline. One in three girls said that they did not want to attend school because of their harassment, while only one in eight boys said they felt similarly. In plain terms, the AAUW found that the effect of sexual harassment on boys was much milder than the effect of the same behavior on girls.

In the workplace, the effects of sexual harassment on men are even less obvious. While one in ten women have had to change jobs due to sexual harassment, fewer than one in a hundred men have had to do so. Men also feel like they have control over incidents of harassment. For example, one man reported this unlikely experience of harassment: "There was a female apprentice that continually made advances. . . . Many of the guys laughed and I began to get real tired of it. I finally had a good man to woman talk and she quit."[81] This man did experience sexual harassment, but the harassment had no significant effect on his employment or in his life.

The sexual harassment of men by women

Nevertheless, a few men have experienced unwelcome sexual conduct at work and suffered because of it. For example, David Papa was seriously and repeatedly sexually harassed while he worked as a manager for Domino's Pizza. When the area supervisor for Domino's, Beth Carrier, visited the store, she took the opportunity to make crude sexual advances toward Papa. She told him that he had a "nice ass," she touched him against his wishes, she pinched his behind, and she made comments about Papa's failing marriage. Papa was embarrassed by Carrier's advances. He rejected them and asked another employee at the store to stay nearby when Carrier visited. Papa did not want to be left alone with her. Ultimately, Carrier's pressure led to a confrontation. Papa told Carrier that he might report her behavior to a supervisor. Carrier told Papa that she would "get him." A week later, Papa was fired.

In a case such as Papa's, where a man suffers serious or repeated sexual harassment from female coworkers or a female supervisor, male employees have the same recourse to

David Papa holds up a copy of the judgment awarding him $237,000 in a case involving sexual harassment by a female supervisor.

the law as female employees. Papa filed an official sexual harassment complaint with the Equal Employment Opportunity Commission (EEOC). His friends did not really understand the situation. "Why didn't you just sleep with her?" they asked him.[82] Nevertheless, the EEOC investigated and found that his claim met the legal standards of sexual harassment. Recognizing the severity of Papa's complaint, the EEOC assigned its own legal staff to the case, and, on behalf of Papa, the commission filed a lawsuit.

Papa's lawsuit had all of the elements of a typical sexual harassment claim. He was repeatedly pressured for dates by a supervisor of the opposite sex. He was physically intimidated. He had clearly felt the effects of his harassment, expressed by his request for support from another employee. Further, Papa was fired for rejecting his supervisor's advances. The court that heard Papa's case found easily in his favor.

Same-sex sexual harassment

Although courts do not often see cases like Papa's, where a man is seriously and repeatedly harassed by a female supervisor, they have no problem handling such a claim. If all of the men who were severely sexually harassed at work brought similar claims to the courtroom, there would be no question that the legal system offers a remedy to men who are seriously harassed. However, in a series of recent lawsuits, a few men have challenged the courts to understand a different kind of sexual harassment—the sexual harassment of men by other men.

At a conservative estimate, approximately one out of every five men who experience sexual harassment at work are sexually harassed by other men. One recent study conducted by researchers at the University of Illinois indicated a much higher number—more than half of the men who reported experiencing sexual harassment had been harassed by other men.

Not "masculine" enough

Sometimes, the Illinois study reports, men are harassed by other men for not being "masculine" enough. One worker in the study described his experience at work with men: "I have felt harassed by . . . the expectation from other men that I will accept and participate in jokes and comments about women," he admitted. Another explained what happened when he tried to take time off from work to care for his children. "Comments were made," he complained. "It made me feel like I wasn't a 'man' if I choose to stay home and take care of the kids." Instead of taking off the three weeks that he had planned, this man could only stay home half that time—one week and two days. "My work wasn't being covered" by the other men, he explained.[83] This type of male-to-male harassment, meant to pressure men into acting in "masculine" ways, can occasionally be serious or repeated enough to interfere with a man's job. A few men have taken complaints of this type to the courts.

Anthony Goluszek is one of those men. Goluszek rarely dated, and he lived at home with his mother. Apparently, this was enough for his coworkers to single him out for harassment. Goluszek testified that his coworkers regularly taunted him. They asked him, in vulgar terms, if he had lately performed sex and informed him, again in crude language, that they would find a woman to have sex with him. Goluszek's coworkers made him the butt of their jokes, he testified, and flaunted pornography at work in an effort to intimidate and humiliate him. They also poked him in the buttocks with a stick, he maintained.

Goluszek repeatedly complained to the supervisor, foreman Bill Clemente, but Clemente took no action. When a female worker at the same company had complained of sexual harassment—several years beforehand—the company had issued a letter warning those involved against further harassment. But Goluszek was expected to live with daily harassment. On several occasions, Goluszek protested, coworkers threatened ominously to knock him off of his ladder with their jeeps. Ultimately, he stopped showing up to work.

Goluszek took his case to court, claiming that he had been singled out for harassment because he was a man. No woman would have been harassed in such a manner, he contended. Further, Goluszek argued that the workers would have been reprimanded if a woman had complained of their conduct. He produced as evidence the company's positive response to the female worker who had been harassed.

The district court that heard his case, however, disagreed with Goluszek's arguments. Goluszek could not claim that he had faced sex discrimination, the court declared. He was "a male in a male-dominated environment," the court declared.[84] A man could not be sexually harassed by other men, reasoned the court. To rule otherwise would be to stretch the law to an absurd limit.

The sex of the harasser is irrelevant

The Equal Employment Opportunity Commission (EEOC), takes a different position on the sexual harassment of men by other men. Same-sex harassment, the EEOC believes, should be illegal.

To make its argument, the EEOC points out that sexual harassment is a type of sex discrimination, and that a supervisor certainly does not have to be of the opposite sex to

discriminate against an employee. For example, if a male executive posts a job advertisement for a secretary with the words "Women Only," the male executive is discriminating against other men. If a female manager announces that she is only considering men for promotion, the female manager is discriminating against other women. In these instances, the discrimination is no less unlawful because the person who is discriminating is of the same sex as the person being discriminated against. The sex of the discriminating person is irrelevant.

In sexual harassment cases, the EEOC maintains, the sex of the harasser should be equally irrelevant. "The crucial inquiry," explains the EEOC, "is whether the harasser treats a member or members of one sex differently from members of the other sex."[85] For the EEOC, the harasser's behavior is the issue at hand, not the harasser's sex.

Many judges agree with the EEOC's position. For example, Judge Loretta A. Preska sided with the EEOC when she handed down her 1995 opinion in *Sardinia v Dellwood*

Foods. "Title VII makes discrimination at the workplace on the basis of [sex] illegal, period," Judge Preska declared in *Sardinia.*[86] "[S]uffering sexual harassment from supervisors of the same sex does nothing to diminish the severity of that harassment."[87]

Not "because of" sex

The Fourth Circuit Court of Appeals, on the other hand, has chosen a middle ground on same-sex harassment. The court has ruled that some same-sex sexual harassment occurs "because of" the employee's sex, and that some same-sex sexual harassment occurs for other reasons. For example, the court dismissed the case of Mark McWilliams, an auto mechanic, who was seriously and repeatedly harassed by his male coworkers. Besides verbal taunts and sexual jokes, such as putting a condom in his food, McWilliams's coworkers physically assaulted him. They tied him up, blindfolded him, and placed a finger in his mouth simulating an act of sex. On another occasion, one coworker stuck McWilliams in the anus with a broom, while another exposed his penis.

When the Fourth Circuit Court heard McWilliams's case, the court focused on the reasons why the harassers behaved as they did. The harassers may have engaged in their behavior because of "the victim's known . . . prudery, or shyness" and because of "their vulgarity and insensitivity and meanness of spirit," the court held.[88] However, the coworkers did not, in the court's opinion, harass McWilliams because of his sex.

The court made this judgment based on its understanding that the harassers were heterosexuals. When heterosexual men harass other men, the court held, they are not motivated by the sex of the man involved. In essence, the court agreed with the reasoning in the earlier case of Anthony Goluszek. McWilliams was a man in a male-dominated environment, the court believed. He was not singled out because of his sex.

Only months later, the same court heard a similar case. A Pizza Hut employee, Arthur Wrightson, had been sexually harassed by his male coworkers and by his supervisor. The coworkers and supervisor groped Wrightson's genitals. They pinched Wrightson's behind. They "pulled out [his] pants to look down them," and they had told crude stories of gay sex, meant to "embarrass and humiliate" Wrightson.[89]

Judging by sexual orientation

In Wrightson's case, the Fourth Circuit Court found in favor of same-sex harassment. Wrightson "would not have been harassed but for the fact that he is male," the court ruled.[90] The Court made this ruling because the coworkers and supervisor in Wrightson's case were openly gay. Gay men harass another man "because of" the man's sex, the court believed, whereas heterosexual men harass other men for different reasons. The Fourth Circuit Court held that same-sex harassment is illegal if the harassers are gay men, but not illegal if the harassers are heterosexual.

Pamela Papish, editor-in-chief of the *Columbia Human Rights Law Review*, is one of those who see a possible prejudice against gays in the Fourth Circuit's decisions. "[T]hough the behavior complained of by the [sexually harassed employees] may be exactly the same, the [Fourth Circuit] approach to same-sex sexual harassment only offers a remedy when the defendant [harasser] is clearly homosexual," she points out.[91] Papish finds this even more troubling in light of the fact that federal laws do not protect gay men and lesbians when they are harassed in the workplace. "[N]ext to women," writes Papish, quoting another author on employment discrimination, "the principal targets of workplace harassment and sexual stereotyping are gay people."[92] Gays are not afforded protection by federal courts, Papish notes, but under the Fourth Circuit Court ruling, they are reproved for behavior that is tolerated in heterosexual men.

In the *New Republic*, Joseph Landau criticizes the Fourth Circuit ruling for a different reason—the burden it places on a sexually harassed worker. "For same-sex cases, this requires proving homosexuality, a nearly impossible burden," he protests.[93]

Nevertheless, other courts have handed down similar decisions. In a 1996 case in Alabama, a district court held:

> In a situation where a male sexually harasses a female, there is the presumption that he does so because she is a female and that he would not do the same to a male. The same is true when a homosexual . . . male harasses another male. . . . However, in the case of same-sex heterosexual . . . sexual harassment, sex discrimination ceases to exist."[94]

The Fifth Circuit and Joseph Oncale

Meanwhile, the Fifth Circuit Court of Appeals has solved the issue of trying to tell gay harassment apart from heterosexual harassment by ruling that same-sex sexual harassment is never a valid legal claim. "Same-sex harassment claims are not viable under Title VII [of the Civil Rights Act of 1964]," the Fifth Circuit has decided.[95] The Fifth Circuit, therefore, does not accept any cases of same-sex sexual harassment.

Although such judicial decisions do not affect most of the public, for Joseph Oncale, the Fifth Circuit Court's position was devastating. Oncale filed his lawsuit after quitting his job on an offshore oil rig in the Gulf of Mexico. According to Oncale's testimony, he worked every day in fear of being sexually violated. More than once, he claims, his supervisor and two of his coworkers physically assaulted him. The coworkers held him down, he says, while the supervisor placed his penis on Oncale's neck. He tells of one time when a coworker held him in the shower while his supervisor pushed a bar of soap into his anus. On several other occasions, Oncale states bluntly, his coworker and supervisor threatened to rape him.

Oncale's lawsuit had all of the elements of sexual harassment. If his testimony could be believed, his supervisor and coworkers used sex to intimidate Oncale, and they molested Oncale on the job. Oncale's lawsuit, however, was filed in Louisiana, a region under the Fifth Circuit Court of Appeals, and the Fifth Circuit has denied his claim. In its ruling, the court sounded almost reluctant because it had already ruled that same-sex harassment is never legally actionable:

> This panel . . . cannot review the merits of [Oncale's] argument on a clean slate. We are bound by our decision in *Garcia v. Elf Atochem No. Am.* [a decision delivered two years earlier stating that same-sex sexual harassment is never legally actionable]. . . . In this Circuit, one panel may not overrule the decision, right or wrong, of a prior panel.[96]

The Supreme Court hears arguments

Oncale appealed the Fifth Circuit's decision, and his appeal was taken up by the Supreme Court. Several prominent legal groups banded together to support Oncale's claim. A brief submitted on behalf of Oncale by a lesbian and gay rights group, the Lambda Legal Defense and Education Fund, was joined by the American Civil Liberties Union (ACLU), the NOW Legal Defense and Education Fund, the National Women's Law Center, the National Center for Lesbian Rights, and People for the American Way. The brief argued that it should not matter, in sexual harassment cases, "whether the harasser's intentions are amorous or hostile."[97] Further, the sex and sexual orientation of the harasser is irrelevant, the groups maintained. Also irrelevant, they contended, is the sexual orientation of the harassed employee.

The brief referred to the Seventh Circuit Court of Appeals, which has taken a broad approach to the issue of same-sex sexual harassment. The Seventh Circuit has written,

> We have difficulty imagining when harassment of this kind would not be . . . "because of" the [harassed employee's] sex. [W]hen one's genitals are grabbed, when one is denigrated in gender-specific language, and when one is threatened with sexual assault, it would seem impossible to de-link the harassment from the [sex] of the individual harassed.[98]

On March 4, 1998, the U.S. Supreme Court ruled that federal law protects employees from sexual harassment in the workplace by people of the same sex. The Supreme Court ruling is of the utmost importance to men who endure serious and repeated same-sex harassment in the workplace or in educational settings. Before this ruling, a man's chances of receiving a favorable verdict depended on the state in which he filed the lawsuit or even the courtroom where his case was heard. In some states, two men who endured the same treatment at work found that their chances of winning a lawsuit depended chiefly on who harassed them, instead of on whether the harassment met the severe or pervasive judicial standard. The Supreme Court ruling has settled many of the issues surrounding same-sex harassment. Foremost among these is the Court's view that the conduct itself, not the sex or motivation of the people involved, determines whether a claim of sexual harassment constitutes sex discrimination, which is prohibited by law.

Joseph Oncale's harassment claim was denied by the Fifth Circuit Court of Appeals because his harassers were male.

6

Speaking Out

A SILENCE SURROUNDS incidents of sexual harassment. Most sexual harassment is never reported, even serious instances of assault and sexual coercion. In the military, at least 60 percent of the sexual harassment of female soldiers goes unreported, and only 17 percent of the sexually harassed male soldiers report their harassment. The Office of Civil Rights in the Department of Education receives no more than a few hundred charges of sexual harassment from students each year, but, according to the comprehensive 1993 American Association of University Women survey of secondary schools, more than one in eight girls report being "forced to do something sexual other than kissing" while at school. Among federal workers, according to statistics released in 1995, only 13 percent of the female employees choose to speak to a supervisor or other official when they experience sexual harassment on the job. Today, there are published procedures within each of these settings for stepping forward with complaints of sexual harassment. But most of the people who experience sexual harassment choose not to speak out.

To some extent, the silence around sexual harassment began to break in October 1991, when law professor Anita Hill came forward with an account of her own sexual harassment, as she remembered it, at the hands of her former supervisor Clarence Thomas. At the time, Thomas was under review as a nominee to the U.S. Supreme Court. Because Hill's account involved a public figure, it received widespread publicity, and the hearings investigating the matter were broadcast live on the ABC, NBC, and CBS television networks.

Thomas vigorously denied Hill's allegations, and he would ultimately be confirmed to the Court, but not before the public watched Professor Hill do something that was rarely done—speak out publicly about her own alleged harassment. Hill's testimony moved other women to come forward with descriptions of their experiences with sexual harassment, and, in the year that followed, sexual harassment became an issue of public debate.

As a direct result of Anita Hill's testimony, more people came forward with charges of sexual harassment than ever before. In 1991, approximately six thousand people filed an official charge of workplace sexual harassment with the Equal Employment Opportunity Commission (EEOC). In 1992, that figure increased by more than 50 percent, and, by 1996, the number of official sexual harassment charges lodged with the EEOC had more than doubled. Moreover, during the same period, official charges of sexual harassment in educational settings more than tripled.

Clarence Thomas was accused of sexual harassment in 1991 by a former colleague, law professor Anita Hill.

Nevertheless, even in the late 1990s, most people who experience sexual harassment remain silent. As late as 1997, Bernice R. Sandler, an expert on sexual harassment in higher education, reported that "the vast majority of women are reluctant to . . . tell anyone in a position to help them, even when serious harassment has occurred."[99] Often, only close friends and family hear about incidents of sexual harassment. Sometimes, nobody is told.

Blaming the victim

Why is it hard for people to speak out against their own sexual harassment? The answer to this question lies not so much in the targets of sexual harassment themselves, but in the behavior of those around them. People do not speak out because they are unsure of the support they will receive from others. The silence around sexual harassment is enforced by society.

How does society contribute to the silence around sexual harassment? One way is by blaming the targets of sexual harassment for the behavior of their harassers.

People who experience sexual harassment can be blamed in many ways. Sometimes, a person who speaks out against sexual harassment is told that she encouraged the harasser by wearing provocative clothing or by acting "too sexually." Research on sexual harassment shows that people are not sexually harassed because of their clothes or their sexuality. Two out of three girls in secondary school are sexually harassed often or occasionally, at least two out of five working women experience sexual harassment on the job, and more than half of the women in the military are harassed in a single year. Even boys and men are occasionally sexually

harassed. Harassment therefore occurs to all types of people, regardless of age or appearance, in all manner of dress. Nevertheless, many people are either unaware of this information or they choose to ignore it, and they are quick to evaluate the targets of harassment for their sexuality. The targets of harassment, they often insist, must have encouraged their harassment by acting "sexually."

The "blame the victim" attitude is widespread among the public, women and men alike. In one *Time* magazine survey, 49 percent of the women and 53 percent of the men polled insisted that women who were sexually harassed had somehow asked for trouble. When people are sexually harassed, they sometimes choose to remain silent because they expect to be blamed or evaluated if they speak out. It may seem easier to remain silent than to face public scrutiny. In this way, blaming the victim serves to keep people from stepping forward with charges of sexual harassment.

Reports are not believed

Blaming the targets for their own harassment is one way that the reaction of others keeps people silent when they are sexually harassed. People do not want to step forward if they are going to be the subject of sexual gossip. Another reason people do not speak out when they are sexually harassed is that they do not always expect to be believed or taken seriously.

In one example, a fourteen-year-old girl who was regularly grabbed by boys on the school bus and taunted with crude sexual insults and slurs tried to report her harassment to the principal. "I told my principal what was happening," she explains. "He was very skeptical about the whole thing, and he didn't do much about it."[100] In another typical instance, a group of middle school girls attempted to report their teacher for groping them only to be accused of inventing their accusations to cause trouble.

Why would people be disbelieved when they step forward with an account of sexual harassment? Little research has been done around this question. Nevertheless, it is generally understood that the public has an exaggerated belief in the possibility of false sexual harassment claims. People are often skeptical when they hear a charge of sexual harassment, as if there were a good possibility that the charge might not be true. Studies show that less than 1 percent of sexual harassment claims involve false accusations, which means that there will be more than ninety-nine real accounts of sexual harassment for every one invented claim. Nevertheless, people often act as if every claim of sexual harassment is suspect.

At least a few of the people who do not report their harassment choose to remain silent because they fear that they will be accused of lying. Who wants to speak out if they feel that they will have to fight simply to be believed?

People who speak out face hostility from others

People who experience sexual harassment also decide not to speak out because they fear that they will face hostility from others if they do so. People who speak out against harassment are often labeled troublemakers and subsequently become unpopular.

There are countless stories of hostility leveled against those who speak out against their own harassment. Margaret Jensvold's coworkers stopped talking to her, for example, when she filed a sexual harassment charge with the EEOC due to the rampant discrimination and sexism which she allegedly encountered at the National Institute of Mental Health. Incredibly, industrial worker Tammy Miller's coworkers also stopped talking to her for reporting three men who held her down and bit her on the behind until she bled. These women had every right to speak out, and should have received support from their coworkers. Instead, they faced hostility.

Why do people who come forward bear such ill-will from others? According to sexual harassment researchers Barbara Gutek and Mary Koss, "[w]orkers who allege harassment are whistle-blowers and, as the carrier of bad news, may be blamed for 'causing trouble.'"[101]

Besides general hostility, people who speak out against sexual harassment have also been known to face serious retaliation. More than a few people have received death threats for speaking out against harassment, and others have had their homes, cars, or offices vandalized. Although these are clearly extreme cases, such forms of retaliation occur more often than most people would imagine.

People who speak out need the support of others

The barriers to speaking out against harassment have proven extremely effective in silencing many of those who would otherwise have come forward. According to statistics released in 1995, 29 percent of the sexually harassed federal workers who chose not to pursue formal action reported that they thought stepping forward would make their work situation "unpleasant." Seventeen percent thought that it would "adversely affect" their careers. Eleven percent reported that they were "too embarrassed" to proceed with formal action, 9 percent thought that they "would be

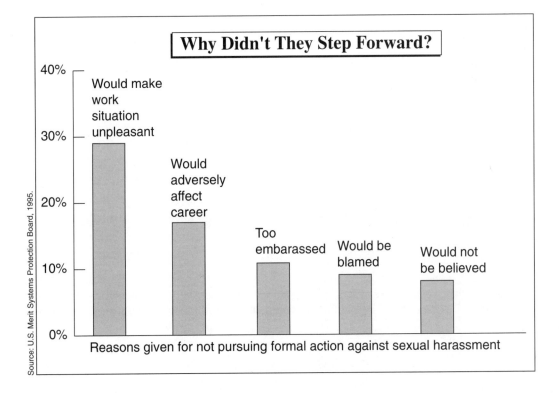

blamed," and 8 percent stated: "Did not think I would be believed."[102] Nearly identical statistics are reported in the military among the female personnel who choose not to report their harassment. The disbelief, hostility, and blame that the targets of sexual harassment expect to receive from others serves as a mechanism for silencing them.

When people remain silent, their harassment almost always continues, and it can often lead to consequences even more serious than the consequences of speaking out. For this reason, sexual harassment experts recommend that those who experience sexual harassment seek out the help of others. Nevertheless, if people are expected to step forward, experts recognize, they will need some assurances that they will be believed and supported. Presently, people do not have those assurances.

Breaking the silence

The progress that the nation has made against sexual harassment can be directly attributed to the women and men

Anita Hill's sexual harassment claim motivated others to come forward with reports of harasssment. Such exposure of the problem is vital to eliminating sexual harassment.

who have chosen to speak out against their own harassment—whatever the personal cost. Justice Department employee Diane Williams moved forward with a sexual harassment lawsuit against all odds and became the first woman to win such a case. Anita Hill appeared on national television with her account of sexual harassment and encouraged others to step forward. Lieutenant Paula Coughlin sacrificed her career as a naval officer to break the silence surrounding sexual harassment in the military. The perseverance of these women cannot be overestimated. They faced considerable resistance, blame, and hostility for speaking out, but they also effected change.

Christine Franklin is another person who spoke out against sexual harassment and effected change. In her case, she changed the law surrounding the sexual harassment of students at school.

While attending the North Gwinnett High School in Gwinnett County, Georgia, Franklin faced continual sexual harassment from a teacher and coach at her high school. The harassment began in the autumn of her tenth-grade year and lasted into the eleventh grade. According to Franklin's account, the harassing teacher asked Franklin about her sexual experiences with her boyfriend and "whether she would consider having sexual intercourse with an older man." He also kissed Franklin against her will while they were in the school parking lot, called Franklin at home to ask her out, and, several times during Franklin's junior year, pulled Franklin out of class, took her to his office, and forced himself on her sexually.[103]

Franklin alerted school officials to the teacher's harassment, and the school investigated the teacher's conduct. During their investigation, however, school officials reportedly took no action to stop the teacher's continuing harassment toward Franklin. They also "discouraged Franklin from pressing charges" against the teacher. The school wished to keep the matter quiet. Ultimately, school officials allowed the teacher to resign "on the condition that all matters pending against him be dropped."[104] Without further pursuing the matter, the school closed its investigation.

A student's persistence pays off

Franklin did not follow the school's lead in letting the matter drop. A few months after the teacher's resignation, Franklin lodged an official charge of sexual harassment with the Office of Civil Rights (OCR). Unfortunately, Franklin found out how ineffective the OCR could be. After several months of investigation, the OCR found that Franklin had indeed been subjected to both physical and verbal sexual harassment while at school, and the school, moreover, had interfered with Franklin's right to complain. However, noting that the teacher in question and another school official involved in the matter had already resigned and the school had created a grievance procedure for sexual harassment complaints, the OCR concluded that there was nothing else that needed to be done. According to the OCR, the school was in the clear.

Franklin refused to accept this dismissal of her charge. She took her case to court, arguing that the school should be forced to pay her damages for the severe abuse that she had endured while attending school—abuse that the school had chosen to ignore. But the district court that heard Franklin's case was unsympathetic. No monetary damage awards were available to students who faced sexual harassment in school, the court held. Unlike employees who could plead lost paychecks because of sexual harassment on the job, sexually harassed students had not lost money and therefore could not be rewarded monetary damages through legal action. Franklin appealed her case to the Second Circuit Court of Appeals. The Second Circuit, however, affirmed the lower court's dismissal. Franklin could not collect monetary damages for the school's negligence in a sexual harassment lawsuit, the court maintained.

Undaunted by this second ruling against her, Franklin appealed her case to the Supreme Court, and the Court took on her appeals. The Supreme Court heard arguments in *Franklin v Gwinnett County Public Schools* on December 11, 1991, and handed down its unanimous decision in favor of Franklin on February 26, 1992. The Supreme Court held that students had a right to seek monetary compensation for the sexual harassment that they endure in school.

Making progress

Franklin's lawsuit resulted in the expansion of legal rights for every student who faces sexual harassment in school. Through her perseverance and diligence, Franklin obtained justice not only for herself, but for students everywhere in the nation. Today, schools are on notice that they can suffer financial losses if they allow sexual harassment to continue. Much of the progress that has been made concerning sexual harassment in school can be directly attributed to this fact.

Franklin's case is a story of serious sexual harassment occurring in a high school. It is also the story of a cover-up by school officials, who attempted to beg Franklin off of lodging official charges. But, most notably, it is the story of a high school student who refused to be silenced and who sought justice all the way to the U.S. Supreme Court. Franklin spoke up, and she made a difference.

Today, sexual harassment is a problem with a name. Now that sexual harassment has been identified, people are speaking out against harassment. There are formidable obstacles to coming forward with an account of sexual harassment. Nevertheless, some people have chosen to come forward regardless of these obstacles, and, because of them, the nation has made progress towards eliminating sexual harassment.

Notes

Introduction

1. Quoted in U.S. Army, "Army Investigates Allegations of Sexual Misconduct and Rape in Training Command," News Release No. 96-78. Army Public Affairs, Washington, DC, November 7, 1996. Available from www.dtic.mil/armylink /news/Nov1996/r19961107apg; Internet.

2. U.S. Department of Education Office for Civil Rights, "Sexual Harassment: It's Not Academic," March 1997, p. 1.

Chapter 1: Sexual Harassment and the Law

3. Quoted in Adele M. Stan, ed., *Debating Sexual Correctness*. New York: Dell Publishing, 1995, p. 4.

4. Quoted in Stan, *Debating Sexual Correctness*, p. 3.

5. *Redbook*, "How Do You Handle Sex on the Job?" January 1976, p. 74.

6. Catharine A. MacKinnon, *Sexual Harassment of Working Women*. New Haven, CT: Yale University Press, 1979, p. 26.

7. Quoted in Stan, *Debating Sexual Correctness*, p. 6.

8. *Williams v Saxbe*, 413 F. Supp. 654 (1976), at 657.

9. *Williams v Saxbe*, at 655.

10. *Bundy v Jackson*, 641 F. 2d 934 (1981), at 940.

11. *Bundy v Jackson*, at 943–944.

12. *Henson v City of Dundee*, 682 F. 2d 897 (1982), at 902.

13. *Henson v City of Dundee*, at 902.

14. Equal Employment Opportunity Commission, Notice 915-050, "Policy Guidance on Current Issues of Sexual Harassment," March 19, 1990, p. 16.

15. *Coley v Consolidated Rail Corp.*, 561 F. Supp. 645 (1982), at 647.

16. *Gan v Kepro Circuit Systems*, 28 FEP Cases 639 (1982), at 641.

17. *Meritor Savings Bank v Vinson*, 477 U.S. 57 (1986), at 67. Chief Justice Rehnquist was quoting an earlier decision, *Henson v City of Dundee*, handed down by the Eleventh Circuit Court of Appeals in 1982.

18. Equal Employment Opportunity Commission, "Guidelines on Discrimination Because of Sex," July 1, 1994, 29 C.F.R. §1604.11.

19. Equal Employment Opportunity Commission, "Guidelines on Discrimination Because of Sex."

Chapter 2: Sexual Harassment in the Workplace

20. Quoted in Amber Coverdale Sumrall and Dena Taylor, eds., *Sexual Harassment: Women Speak Out*. Freedom, CA: Crossing Press, 1992, pp. 156–57.

21. Quoted in Celia Morris, *Bearing Witness: Sexual Harassment and Beyond—Everywoman's Story*. Boston: Little, Brown, 1994, p. 75.

22. *People Weekly*, "A Startling Study Claims that Sexual Harassment in the Office is as Common as the Coffee Break," June 8, 1981, p. 123.

23. Quoted in Michele A. Paludi and Richard B. Barickman, *Academic and Workplace Sexual Harassment*. Albany: State University of New York Press, 1991, p. 138.

24. Ronni Sandroff, "Sexual Harassment in the Fortune 500," *Working Woman*, December, 1988, p. 71.

25. Sandroff, "Sexual Harassment in the Fortune 500," p. 72.

26. Peter Rutter, *Sex, Power, and Boundaries*. New York: Bantam Books, 1996, p. 145.

27. Quoted in Ellen Bravo and Ellen Cassedy, *The 9 to 5 Guide to Combating Sexual Harassment*. New York: John Wiley & Sons, 1992, p. 102.

28. Quoted in Diane K. Shrier, ed., *Sexual Harassment in the Workplace and Academia: Psychiatric Issues*. Washington, DC: American Psychiatric Press, 1996, pp. 135, 143.

29. *New York Times*, "Excerpts from the Supreme Court Ruling on a Lawsuit Against Clinton," May 28, 1997, p. A16.

30. Catherine Yang, "Getting Justice Is No Easy Task," *Business Week*, May 13, 1996, p. 98.

31. Quoted in Alexandra Alger and William G. Flanagan, "Sexual Politics," *Forbes*, May 6, 1996, p. 106.

Chapter 3: Sexual Harassment in Education

32. American Association of University Women Educational Foundation, *Hostile Hallways: The AAUW Survey on Sexual Harassment in America's Schools*. Washington, DC: American Association of University Women Educational Foundation, 1993.

33. American Association of University Women Educational Foundation, *Hostile Hallways,* pp. 3, 4.

34. Quoted in Nan Stein, *Secrets in Public: Sexual Harassment in Public (and Private) Schools*. Wellesley, MA: Center for Research on Women, 1992, p. 13.

35. U.S. Department of Education Office of Civil Rights, "Sexual Harassment: It's Not Academic," p. 2.

36. Quoted in Nan Stein and Lisa Sjostrom, *Flirting or Hurting? A Teacher's Guide on Student-to-Student Sexual Harassment in Schools*. Washington, DC: National Education Association, 1994, p. 89.

37. Quoted in Stein, *Secrets in Public*, p. 5.

38. Stein and Sjostrom, *Flirting or Hurting?* p. 96.

39. Susan Strauss with Pamela Espeland, *Sexual Harassment and Teens*. Minneapolis: Free Spirit Publishing, 1992, p. 7.

40. Stein and Sjostrom, *Flirting or Hurting?* p. v.

41. Stein and Sjostrom, *Flirting or Hurting?* p. 56.

42. Stein and Sjostrom, *Flirting or Hurting?* p. 101.

43. Quoted in Adam Nossiter, "Six-Year-Old's Sex Crime: Innocent Peck on Cheek," *New York Times*, September 27, 1996, p. A14.

44. Quoted in Norimitsu Onishi, "Harassment in 2d Grade? Queens Kisser Is Pardoned," *New York Times*, October 3, 1996, p. A1.

45. Quoted in Inara Verzemnieks, "When Children Kiss," *Washington Post*, October 11, 1996, p. D5.

46. U.S. Department of Education Office of Civil Rights, "Sexual Harassment Guidance: Harassment of Students by

School Employees, Other Students, or Third Parties; Notice," March 13, 1997. Federal Register, vol. 62, no. 49, p. 12034.

47. Quoted in Kathlyn Gay, *Rights and Respect: What You Need to Know About Gender Bias and Sexual Harassment.* Brookfield, CT: Millbrook Press, 1995, p. 67.

48. Quoted in Stein and Sjostrom, *Flirting or Hurting?* p. 103.

49. Bernice R. Sandler and Robert J. Shoop, eds., *Sexual Harassment on Campus.* Boston: Allyn & Bacon, 1997, p. 104.

50. Quoted in Sandler and Shoop, eds., *Sexual Harassment on Campus*, p. 266.

51. U.S. Department of Education Office of Civil Rights, "Sexual Harassment Guidance," pp. 12045, 12046.

52. *Silva v University of New Hampshire*, 888 F. Supp. 293 (1994), at 78.

53. Quoted in Sandler and Shoop, eds., *Sexual Harassment on Campus*, p. 282.

Chapter 4: Sexual Harassment in the Military

54. Quoted in U.S. Army, "Army Investigates Allegations of Sexual Misconduct and Rape in Training Command."

55. Quoted in *Online Newshour*, "Army Sex Scandal: Improper Conduct," Transcript, December 26, 1996. Available from www.pbs.org/newshour/bb/military/army_12-26; Internet.

56. Quoted in *CNN Interactive*, "Calls Still Pouring In on Army Harassment Hot Line," November 17, 1996. Available from www.cnn.com/us/9611/17/military.sex/index; Internet.

57. Department of Defense, "Summary of Department of Defense 1995 Sexual Harassment Study," July 2, 1996. Available from www.defenselink.mil/news/fact_sheets/sxhas95; Internet.

58. Department of Defense, "1995 Sexual Harassment Survey," News Release No. 410-96, Office of Assistant Secretary of Defense (Public Affairs), Washington, DC, July 2, 1996. Available from www.defenselink.mil/news/Jul1996/b070296_bt410-96; Internet.

59. Quoted in Jean Zimmerman, *Tailspin: Women at War in the Wake of Tailhook.* New York: Doubleday, 1995, p. 79.

60. Quoted in Ellen Goodman, *Value Judgments*. New York: Farrar, Straus & Giroux, 1993, p. 75.

61. Quoted in Eric Schmitt, "Navy Says Dozens of Women Were Harassed at Pilots Convention," *New York Times*, May 1, 1992, p. A14.

62. Quoted in Zimmerman, *Tailspin*, p. 27.

63. Patrick B. Pexton, "Military Injustice: 'Zero Tolerance' Makes Zero Sense When It Applies Only to the Lower Ranks," *Washington Post*, May 19, 1997, p. C7.

64. Department of Defense, "Summary of Department of Defense 1995 Sexual Harassment Study."

65. Quoted in *Online Newshour*, "Army Sex Scandal: Improper Conduct."

66. Zimmerman, *Tailspin*, p. 14.

67. Zimmerman, *Tailspin*, p. 270.

68. Quoted in *Online Newshour*, "Harassment in the Military," Transcript, February 4, 1997. Available from www.pbs.org/newshour/bb/military/jan-june97 /harassment_2-4; Internet.

69. Quoted in *Online Newshour*, "Marching Side by Side," Transcript, April 30, 1997. Available from www.pbs.org /newshour/bb/military/april97/coed_4-30; Internet.

70. CMR Notes, "CMR Calls for Army Secretary Togo West to Resign," 33, October/November 1997, p. 1.

71. *Washington Post*, "Women in the Military," May 1, 1997, p. A22.

72. Jeanne Holm, *Women in the Military: An Unfinished Revolution*. Novato, CA: Presidio Press, 1992, p. 393.

73. Holm, *Women in the Military*, p. 384.

74. Department of Defense, "Gender Integrated Training," June 3, 1997, News Briefing, Office of the Assistant Secretary of Defense (Public Affairs), Washington, DC. Available from www.defenselink.mil/news/Jun1997/x06051997_x0603gen; Internet.

75. Quoted in Eric Schmitt, "Role of Women in the Military Is Again Bringing Debate," *New York Times*, December 29, 1996, p. A14.

76. Department of Defense, "Gender Integrated Training."

77. Department of Defense, "Secretary of Defense Statement on Sexual Harassment in the Army," News Release No. 475-97, Office of Assistant Secretary of Defense (Public Affairs), Washington, DC, September 11, 1997. Available from www.defenselink.mil/news/Sep1997/b09111997_bt475-97; Internet.

78. Quoted in Philip Shenon, "Army's Leadership Blamed in Report on Sexual Abuse," *New York Times*, September 12, 1997, p. A1.

Chapter 5: What About Men?

79. Quoted in Jennifer L. Berdahl, Vicki J. Magley, and Craig R. Waldo, "The Sexual Harassment of Men?" *Psychology of Women Quarterly*, 20 (1996), pp. 538–39.

80. Quoted in Berdahl, Magley, and Waldo, "The Sexual Harassment of Men?" p. 541.

81. Quoted in Berdahl, Magley, and Waldo, "The Sexual Harassment of Men?" p. 541.

82. Quoted in *Time*, "My Friends Were Like, 'Why Didn't You Just Sleep with Her?'" December 4, 1995, p. 22.

83. Quoted in Berdahl, Magley, and Waldo, "The Sexual Harassment of Men?" p. 540.

84. *Goluszek v Smith*, 697 F. Supp. 1452 (1988), at 1456.

85. Quoted in *Sardinia v Dellwood Foods*, 69 FEP Cases 705, at 711.

86. *Sardinia v Dellwood Foods*, at 709.

87. *Sardinia v Dellwood Foods*, at 710.

88. Quoted in Pamela J. Papish, "Homosexual Harassment or Heterosexual Horseplay? The False Dichotomy of Same-Sex Sexual Harassment Law," *Columbia Human Rights Law Review*, vol. 28:201, 1996, p. 212.

89. Quoted in Papish, "Homosexual Harassment or Heterosexual Horseplay?" p. 219.

90. Quoted in Papish, "Homosexual Harassment or Heterosexual Horseplay?" p. 219.

91. Papish, "Homosexual Harassment or Heterosexual Horseplay?" p. 219.

92. Papish, "Homosexual Harassment or Heterosexual Horseplay?" p. 220.

93. Joseph Landau, "Out of Order," *New Republic*, May 5, 1997, p. 9.

94. *Martin v Norfolk Southern Railway Co.*, 70 FEP Cases 1723 (1996), at 1726–1727.

95. *Oncale v Sundowner Offshore Services, Inc.*, 83 F. 3d 118 (1996), at 120.

96. *Oncale v Sundowner Offshore Services, Inc.*, at 119.

97. American Civil Liberties Union, "ACLU Urges Supreme Court to Bar Same-Sex Sexual Harassment Under Title VII," ACLU Press Release, August 13, 1997. Available from www.aclu.org/news/n081397a; Internet.

98. Quoted in American Civil Liberties Union, "ACLU Urges Supreme Court to Bar Same-Sex Sexual Harassment Under Title VII."

Chapter 6: Speaking Out

99. Sandler and Shoop, eds., *Sexual Harassment on Campus*, p. 19.

100. Quoted in Stein, *Secrets in Public*, p. 23.

101. Quoted in Shrier, *Sexual Harassment in the Workplace and Academia: Psychiatric Issues*, p. 53.

102. U.S. Merit Systems Protection Board, "Sexual Harassment in the Federal Workplace: Trends, Progress, and Continuing Challenges," p. 35.

103. *Franklin v Gwinnett County Pub. Schs.*, 503 U.S. 60 (1992), at 63.

104. *Franklin v Gwinnett County Pub. Schs.*, at 64.

Organizations
to Contact

American Association of University Women (AAUW)
1111 Sixteenth St. NW
Washington, DC 20036
(202) 785-7700

The AAUW seeks to promote education and equal opportunities for women and girls. As a part of this mission, the AAUW includes an Educational Foundation that funds research on girls and education, community action projects, and fellowships and grants for women in the United States and abroad. The AAUW also includes a Legal Advocacy Fund that offers funds and support for women seeking legal action for sex discrimination in higher education. In 1993, the AAUW Educational Foundation conducted an extensive survey of sexual harassment in the nation's secondary schools. The results of this survey are available in the AAUW publication *Hostile Hallways*.

American Civil Liberties Union (ACLU)
132 W. 43rd St.
New York, NY 10036
(212) 549-2500

Founded in 1920, the ACLU champions the rights of individuals as defined by the Bill of Rights. Although the ACLU is best known for its work in preserving the rights of free speech and freedom of assembly, the ACLU also advocates equal protection under the law for all individuals regardless of race, sex, religion, national origin, sexual orientation, age, physical handicap, or other such classifications. The ACLU has national projects devoted to women's rights, children's rights, workplace rights, and lesbian and gay rights.

American Psychological Association (APA)
750 First St. NE
Washington, DC 20002-4242
(202) 336-5500

The APA is the largest scientific and professional organization representing psychology in the United States. The association offers information on sexual harassment for the public, including a list of public myths about harassment and a description of documented, stress-related effects associated with the experience of sexual harassment. The APA also provides referrals to state and local associations that offer aid to people who are targeted for sexual harassment.

Center for Military Readiness (CMR)
PO Box 51600
Livonia, MI 48151
(313) 464-9430

The Center for Military Readiness was founded to give voice to the problems and concerns of men and women in uniform. As a part of its mission, CMR opposes the inclusion of women into combat positions and the implementation of co-educational basic training. CMR is also concerned with military budget cutbacks and the placement of American troops under international command. The center publishes *CMR Notes*, a monthly newsletter.

Equal Employment Opportunity Commission (EEOC)
1801 L St. NW
Washington, DC 20507
(202) 663-4900

The EEOC is the government agency charged with enforcing federal laws against discrimination in the workplace, which include laws against sexual harassment. The agency publishes detailed guidelines on sexual harassment and the law. The EEOC also represents several dozen sexually harassed employees in court each year and files "friend of the court" briefs in important discrimination cases. Employees who believe that they have encountered serious or repeated sexual harassment in the workplace can lodge an official charge against the employer with the EEOC, which the EEOC may then investigate.

Independent Women's Forum (IWF)
2111 Wilson Blvd., Suite 550
Arlington, VA 22201-3057
(703) 243-8989

The Independent Women's Forum formed in response to the Anita Hill–Clarence Thomas Senate Judiciary Committee hearings. The forum was established by politically conservative women who supported Thomas's nomination. IWF seeks to provide an alternative to feminist organizations by promoting the ethics of individual responsibility, strong families, limited government, and opportunity for all Americans. IWF publishes the *Women's Quarterly* and a newsletter for its members titled *Ex Femina*.

Lambda Legal Defense and Education Fund
120 Wall St., 15th Floor
New York, NY 10005
(212) 809-8585

Founded in 1973, the Lambda Legal Defense and Education Fund is the nation's oldest and largest lesbian and gay rights legal organization. Through its litigation, education, and public policy work, Lambda champions the civil rights of lesbians, gay men, and people with HIV/AIDS. Lambda believes that laws against same-sex sexual harassment should not turn on questions of sexual orientation, and it recently entered a brief in favor of Joseph Oncale, who is bringing a case of same-sex sexual harassment before the U.S. Supreme Court.

Men's Rights, Inc. (MR)
PO Box 163180
Sacramento, CA 93816
(916) 484-7333

MR is dedicated to ending sexism toward men. The group maintains that current sexual harassment laws are weighted in favor of women, and has expressed concern for the rights of men accused of sexual harassment. MR also runs a Media Watch Project, overseeing the portrayal of men in advertising, entertainment, and news coverage; a Pro-Choice for Men Too Project, seeking to give men the same control over parental destiny currently offered to women; and a project aimed at educating the public about the benefits of equality for men.

National Organization for Women (NOW)
1000 16th St. NW, Suite 700
Washington, DC 20036
(202) 331-0066

NOW was established in 1966 to fight for the equality of women and to push for social change, and it is the largest organization of feminist activists in the United States today. The group organizes mass marches, rallies, pickets, counter-demonstrations, and actions of nonviolent civil disobedience. NOW activists also work for political change through legal action and within the electoral system. The organization supports economic equality for women, the passage of the Equal Rights Amendment, the right of reproductive freedom, and an end to racism, bigotry, and violence against women. NOW recently named Smith Barney and Mitsubishi Motors as "merchants of shame" for the alleged sexual harassment that has been reported within those companies.

9 to 5 National Association of Working Women
238 Wisconsin Ave., Suite 700
Milwaukee, WI 53203-2308
(414) 274-0925
Job Problem Hotline: (800) 522-0925

9 to 5 is a nationwide, grassroots organization that provides information and training on sexual harassment. 9 to 5 also runs a hot line for working women who face sexual harassment on the job. In 1992, founder Ellen Cassedy and national director Ellen Bravo coauthored *The 9 to 5 Guide to Combating Sexual Harassment*, a clear and informative look at sexual harassment on the job.

NOW Legal Defense and Education Fund
99 Hudson St., 12th Floor
New York, NY 10013
(212) 925-6635

Established by the National Organization for Women (NOW) as a separate organization, the NOW Legal Defense and Education Fund offers legal referrals and legal support. The fund provides a legal resource kit for targets of sexual harassment as well as sample sexual harassment policies for employers.

U.S. Department of Education Office for Civil Rights (OCR)
330 C St. SW, Mary Switzer Building
Washington, DC 20202-1328
(800) 421-3481

The OCR provides critical services for students and schools. Students, parents, faculty, or school staff who experience or witness serious or repeated sexual harassment have the right to lodge an official charge with the OCR. If the OCR finds reasonable cause, members of the OCR will visit the educational institution for further investigation. The OCR also offers an easy-to-read pamphlet on sexual harassment for school administrators titled *Sexual Harassment: It's Not Academic*, and a legalistic *Guidance* on sexual harassment with more detailed information.

U.S. Merit Systems Protection Board (MSPB)
1120 Vermont Ave. NW, Room 884
Washington, DC 20419
(800) 209-8960

MSPB is an independent agency responsible for protecting the integrity of the civil service. MSPB has conducted extensive surveys of sexual harassment in the federal workplace since 1980. The agency is, therefore, in a rare position to evaluate long-term changes in the workplace with regard to sexual harassment, including changes in the attitudes of federal workers toward sexual harassment, the potential effects of sexual harassment training, and the impact of harassment on both female and male civil servants. MSPB's detailed report on sexual harassment is available to the public upon request.

Women's Legal Defense Fund (WLDF)
1875 Connecticut Ave. NW, Suite 710
Washington, DC 20009
(202) 986-2600

Established in 1971, WLDF's mission is "to make the world a better place for women and their families." WLDF works within the courts, the government, and at the grassroots level to advance equal opportunity and economic security for women, to oppose discrimination against women in employment and education, and to assure women's access to health care and full reproductive health services. WLDF publishes a quarterly newsletter for its members and provides a fact sheet on sexual harassment for the public.

Suggestions for Further Reading

Kathlyn Gay, *Rights and Respect: What You Need to Know About Gender Bias and Sexual Harassment.* Brookfield, CT: Millbrook Press, 1995. A clear and thoughtful presentation of the issues surrounding sexual harassment, including an excellent discussion of gender stereotypes and an informed look at the Anita Hill–Clarence Thomas hearings.

JoAnn Bren Guernsey, *Sexual Harassment: A Question of Power.* Minneapolis: Lerner Publications, 1995. A well-balanced look at the problem of sexual harassment, with discussions on women who work in nontraditional fields, ways to respond to sexual harassment, and a chapter on what the future may bring.

Kim Ratcliffe, "Five Girls Fight Back," *Seventeen*, July 1996. A report on five girls who spoke up against their sexual harassment. Shows the difficulties students face when bringing instances of sexual harassment to light.

Karin L. Swisher, ed., *What Is Sexual Harassment?* San Diego: Greenhaven Press, 1995. A fascinating collection of essays on sexual harassment written by academics, activists, and thinkers. Chapters range from fact-based discussions of the issue to emotional, personal viewpoint editorials.

Leora Tanenbaum, "Bad Reputation," *Seventeen*, January 1997. An insightful look at sexual rumors in high school, told as personal anecdote. Raises the difficult and important issue of young women who sexually harass other young women.

Works Consulted

Alexandra Alger and William G. Flanagan, "Sexual Politics," *Forbes*, May 6, 1996.

American Association of University Women Educational Foundation, *Hostile Hallways: The AAUW Survey on Sexual Harassment in America's Schools*. Washington, DC: American Association of University Women Educational Foundation, 1993.

American Civil Liberties Union, "ACLU Urges Supreme Court to Bar Same-Sex Sexual Harassment Under Title VII," ACLU Press Release, August 13, 1997. Available from www.aclu.org/news/n081397a; Internet.

American Psychological Association Media Information, "Sexual Harassment: Myths and Realities." Available from www.apa.org/pubinfo/harass; Internet.

Jennifer L. Berdahl, Vicki J. Magley, and Craig R. Waldo, "The Sexual Harassment of Men?" *Psychology of Women Quarterly*, 20, 1996.

Ellen Bravo and Ellen Cassedy, *The 9 to 5 Guide to Combating Sexual Harassment*. New York: John Wiley & Sons, 1992.

CMR Notes, "CMR Calls for Army Secretary Togo West to Resign," 33, October/November 1997.

CNN Interactive, "Army Drops Rape Charge Against Aberdeen Drill Instructor," May 27, 1997. Available from www.cnn.com/us/9705/27/; Internet.

———, "Calls Still Pouring in on Army Harassment Hot Line," November 17, 1996. Available from www.cnn.com/us/9611/17/military.sex/index; Internet.

Elsa Kircher Cole, ed., *Sexual Harassment on Campus: A Legal Compendium*. Washington, DC: National Association of College and University Attorneys, 1990.

Department of Defense, "Gender Integrated Training," June 3, 1997, News Briefing, Office of the Assistant Secretary of Defense (Public Affairs), Washington, DC. Available from www.defenselink.mil/news/Jun1997/x06051997_x0603gen; Internet.

———, "1995 Sexual Harassment Survey," July 2, 1996, News Release No. 410-96, Office of Assistant Secretary of Defense (Public Affairs), Washington, DC. Available from www.defenselink.mil/news/Jul1996 /b070296_bt410-96; Internet.

———, "Secretary of Defense Statement on Sexual Harassment in the Army," September 11, 1997, News Release No. 475-97, Office of Assistant Secretary of Defense (Public Affairs), Washington, DC. Available from www.defenselink.mil/news/Sep1997/b09111997_bt475-97; Internet.

———, "Summary of Department of Defense 1995 Sexual Harassment Study," July 2, 1996. Available from www.defenselink.mil/news/fact_sheets /sxhas95; Internet.

Timothy Egan, "Conflict Between Sexes, Not Combat, May Soon Define Modern Army," *New York Times*, November 15, 1996.

Equal Employment Opportunity Commission, "Guidelines on Discrimination Because of Sex," July 1, 1994.

———, Notice 915-050, "Policy Guidance on Current Issues of Sexual Harassment," March 19, 1990.

Susan Faludi, *Backlash*. New York: Crown, 1991.

Lin Farley, *Sexual Shakedown: The Sexual Harassment of Women on the Job*. New York: McGraw-Hill, 1978.

Sarah Glazer, "Crackdown on Sexual Harassment: Is the Nation Overreacting to the Problem?" *CQ Researcher*, July 19, 1996.

Ellen Goodman, *Value Judgments*. New York: Farrar, Straus & Giroux, 1993.

Kirstin Downey Grimsley, "Worker Bias Cases Are Rising Steadily," *Washington Post*, May 12, 1997.

Jeanne Holm, *Women in the Military: An Unfinished Revolution*. Novato, CA: Presidio Press, 1992.

Joseph Landau, "Out of Order," *New Republic*, May 5, 1997.

Catharine A. MacKinnon, *Feminism Unmodified: Discourses on Life and Law*. Cambridge, MA: Harvard University Press. 1987.

————, *Sexual Harassment of Working Women*. New Haven, CT: Yale University Press, 1979.

Joan Magretta, "Will She Fit In?" *Harvard Business Review*, March/April 1997.

Jane Mayer and Jill Abramson, *Strange Justice*. New York: Penguin Books USA, 1994.

Anita Miller, ed., *The Complete Transcripts of the Clarence Thomas–Anita Hill Hearings: October 11, 12, 13, 1991*. Chicago: Academy Chicago Publishers, 1994.

Maureen F. Moore and Jonathan L. Adler, *Sexual Harassment: Discrimination and Other Claims*. Carlsbad, CA: Michie, Parker Publications Division, 1996.

Celia Morris, *Bearing Witness: Sexual Harassment and Beyond—Everywoman's Story*. Boston: Little, Brown, 1994.

National Organization for Women, "Despite Aberdeen Verdict: Military Is Accessory to Abuses Until Outside Investigating Process Is Implemented," Press Release, April 29, 1997. Available from www.now.org/press/04-97/04-29-97; Internet.

————, "NOW Challenges All Branches of the Military to Clean House," Press Release, November 14, 1996. Available from www.now.org/press/11-96/11-14-96; Internet.

New York Times, "Excerpts from the Supreme Court Ruling on a Lawsuit Against Clinton," May 28, 1997.

Adam Nossiter, "Six-Year-Old's Sex Crime: Innocent Peck on Cheek," *New York Times*, September 27, 1996.

Robert M. O'Neil, *Free Speech in the College Community*. Bloomington: Indiana University Press, 1997.

Norimitsu Onishi, "Harassment in 2d Grade? Queens Kisser Is Pardoned," *New York Times*, October 3, 1996.

Online Newshour, "Army Sex Scandal: Improper Conduct," Transcript, December 26, 1996. Available from www.pbs.org/newshour/bb/military/army_12-26; Internet.

————, "Harassment in the Military," Transcript, February 4, 1997. Available from www.pbs.org/newshour/bb/military /jan-june97/harassment_2-4; Internet.

————, "Marching Side by Side," Transcript, April 30, 1997. Available from www.pbs.org/newshour/bb/military /april97/coed_4-30; Internet.

Michele A. Paludi, ed., *Ivory Power: Sexual Harassment on Campus*. Albany: State University of New York Press, 1990.

Michele A. Paludi and Richard B. Barickman, *Academic and Workplace Sexual Harassment*. Albany: State University of New York Press, 1991.

Pamela J. Papish, "Homosexual Harassment or Heterosexual Horseplay? The False Dichotomy of Same-Sex Sexual Harassment Law," *Columbia Human Rights Law Review*, vol. 28:201, 1996.

People Weekly, "A Startling Study Claims that Sexual Harassment in the Office Is as Common as the Coffee Break," June 8, 1981.

William Petrocelli and Barbara Kate Repa, *Sexual Harassment on the Job*. Berkeley, CA: Nolo Press, 1992.

Patrick B. Pexton, "Military Injustice: 'Zero Tolerance' Makes Zero Sense When It Applies Only to the Lower Ranks," *Washington Post*, May 19, 1997.

Redbook, "How Do You Handle Sex on the Job?" January 1976.

Peter Rutter, *Sex, Power, and Boundaries*. New York: Bantam Books, 1996.

Amy Saltzman, "Do You Have the Stamina?" *U.S. News & World Report*, August 19, 1996.

Bernice R. Sandler and Robert J. Shoop, eds., *Sexual Harassment on Campus*. Boston: Allyn & Bacon, 1997.

Ronni Sandroff, "Sexual Harassment in the Fortune 500," *Working Woman*, December 1988.

Kristina Sauerwein, "A New Lesson in Schools: Sexual Harassment Is Unacceptable," *Los Angeles Times*, August 1, 1994.

Eric Schmitt, "Navy Says Dozens of Women Were Harassed at Pilots Convention," *New York Times*, May 1, 1992.

———, "Role of Women in the Military Is Again Bringing Debate," *New York Times*, December 29, 1996.

Philip Shenon, "Army's Leadership Blamed in Report on Sexual Abuse," *New York Times*, September 12, 1997.

Robert J. Shoop and Debra L. Edwards, *How to Stop Sexual Harassment in Our Schools*. Boston: Allyn & Bacon, 1994.

Diane K. Shrier, ed., *Sexual Harassment in the Workplace and Academia: Psychiatric Issues*. Washington, DC: American Psychiatric Press, 1996.

Rosemarie Skaine, *Power and Gender: Issues in Sexual Dominance and Harassment*. Jefferson, NC: McFarland, 1996.

Adele M. Stan, ed., *Debating Sexual Correctness*. New York: Dell Publishing, 1995.

Nan Stein, *Secrets in Public: Sexual Harassment in Public (and Private) Schools*. Wellesley, MA: Center for Research on Women, 1992.

Nan Stein and Lisa Sjostrom, *Flirting or Hurting? A Teacher's Guide on Student-to-Student Sexual Harassment in Schools*. Washington, DC: National Education Association, 1994.

Susan Strauss with Pamela Espeland, *Sexual Harassment and Teens*. Minneapolis: Free Spirit Publishing, 1992.

Amber Coverdale Sumrall and Dena Taylor, eds., *Sexual Harassment: Women Speak Out*. Freedom, CA: Crossing Press, 1992.

Karin L. Swisher, ed., *Sexual Harassment*. San Diego: Greenhaven Press, 1992.

Time, "My Friends Were Like, 'Why Didn't You Just Sleep with Her?'" December 4, 1995.

U.S. Army, "Army Investigates Allegations of Sexual Misconduct and Rape in Training Command," News Release No. 96-78. Army Public Affairs, Washington, DC, November 7, 1996. Available from www.dtic.mil/armylink /news/Nov1996/r19961107apg; Internet.

U.S. Department of Education Office for Civil Rights, "Sexual Harassment Guidance: Harassment of Students by School Employees, Other Students, or Third Parties; Notice," March 13, 1997. Federal Register, vol. 62, no. 49.

———, "Sexual Harassment: It's Not Academic," March 1997.

U.S. Merit Systems Protection Board, "Sexual Harassment in the Federal Workplace: Trends, Progress, and Continuing Challenges," Washington, DC, U.S. Government Printing Office, 1995.

Inara Verzemnieks, "When Children Kiss," *Washington Post*, October 11, 1996.

Washington Post, "Women in the Military," May 1, 1997.

Catherine Yang, "Getting Justice Is No Easy Task," *Business Week*, May 13, 1996.

Jean Zimmerman, *Tailspin: Women at War in the Wake of Tailhook*. New York: Doubleday, 1995.

Legal Cases Cited

Bundy v Jackson, 641 F. 2d 934 (1981).

Coley v Consolidated Rail Corp., 561 F. Supp. 645 (1982).

EEOC v Domino's Pizza, Inc., 69 FEP Cases 570.

Franklin v Gwinnett County Pub. Schs., 503 U.S. 60 (1992).

Gan v Kepro Circuit Systems, 28 FEP Cases 639 (1982).

Goluszek v Smith, 697 F. Supp. 1452 (1988).

Harris v Forklift Systems, 114 S.Ct. 367 (1993).

Henson v City of Dundee, 682 F. 2d 897 (1982).

Martin v Norfolk Southern Railway Co., 70 FEP Cases 1723 (1996).

Meritor Savings Bank v Vinson, 477 U.S. 57 (1986).

Oncale v Sundowner Offshore Services, Inc., 83 F. 3d 118 (1996).

Sardinia v Dellwood Foods, 69 FEP Cases 705 (1995).

Silva v University of New Hampshire, 888 F. Supp. 293 (1994).

Williams v Saxbe, 413 F. Supp. 654 (1976).

Zabkowicz v West Bend Co., 589 F. Supp. 780 (1984).

Index

Picture Credits

About the Author

Keith McGowan travels, writes, and teaches children of all ages. He has lived in Australia, Haiti, and Chile, as well as on both coasts of the United States. He is presently working on a series of picture books for young readers and planning a trip through Asia.

DATE DUE

CHAVEZ HIGH SCHOOL
LIBRARY
HOUSTON, TEXAS